THE **COCKTAIL** BOOK

THE COCKTAIL BOOK

THE COMPLETE GUIDE TO HOME COCKTAILS
BY MICHAEL WALKER

HPBooks

©1980 Michael Walker/London Editions

Designed and produced by London Editions
Limited
9 Long Acre, London WC2E 9LH.
Edited by Janet Sacks
Designed and art directed by Rick Fawcett

Photographs by Robert Golden

First published in hardcover in Great Britain in
1980 by Queen Anne Press, Macdonald Futura
Publishers, Paulton House, 8 Shepherdess Walk,
London N1 7LW.

First published in USA in 1980 by HPBooks®
A Division of HPBooks, Inc.
P.O. Box 5367, Tucson, AZ 85703.
Tel: (602) 888-2150

Library of Congress Catalog number 80-81668

ISBN 0-89586-069-4

Printed by Dong-A Printing Co., Ltd, Seoul,
Korea. Represented by Codra Enterprises
2nd Printing

CONTENTS

Introduction

With the recent revival of cocktails and the 'happy hour', people who frequent the bars of London will have become acutely aware of the lack of expertise displayed by many a barman. It is also true that patrons themselves are often unaware of how to prepare and present the cocktails they enjoy, and display a certain apathy in returning cocktails which have been badly made. Thus there seems to be a need for a book which will not only provide the amateur barman with recipes for cocktails, both popular and less well known, but which will also act as a guide to making them.

When first setting up a bar, it is not wise, even if you can afford it, to buy out the entire liquor store; you need to know which will be the most useful bottles to buy, how to get the most from the least. In this way the cost of your experimenting will be kept to a minimum. It is also necessary to know what equipment you may require, from a measuring cup to a blender, and how to improvise if the right equipment is not available. As the presentation of cocktails is so important the range of glasses and the different garnishes to use is another essential piece of information.

Despite the myriad of concoctions already tried and tested, new recipes are continually cropping up. The more exotic fruits are now easier to find than they were in a big town or city, and, when blended with a variety of liquors, they can make the most delectable cocktails. Recipes flood in from far-flung corners of the world, for today travel is cheaper than ever before. A visitor to a tropical isle is a bonus to his friends when he comes back with ideas for refreshingly different fruit cocktails.

My entrée into the world of cocktails was entirely by chance, despite my training in catering. I was working in one of London's first American-style restaurants in Covent Garden when out of the blue I was offered the chance of being trained as bartender. From the day I stepped behind the bar, a whole new world opened up to me with a language all of its own and I had to learn terms like serving a drink 'straight up', and how to make a perfect 'twist' of lemon. I also learned that a barman need never be still; if there are no customers to serve there is always something to be done, from simple but essential cleaning of the bar to checking of the stock. And, of course, I learned how to mix and experiment with cocktails.

An enthusiastic traveller, I began to collect recipes on my travels. I visited bars in foreign places from Tunisia to Trinidad. Back in London I became Head Barman in the new Peppermint Park which, although not the first cocktail bar, was to make its mark by introducing cocktails to a much wider audience. Its stunning décor enticed the trendsetters and, with its tables permanently filled, it was destined for success.

The staff took great pleasure in explaining to customers how certain cocktails were made and where to buy glasses and bar equipment. I compiled a training manual for the trainee barmen and several customers asked for copies! I realized then that there was a need for a simple but comprehensive book which dealt with every aspect of making cocktails, from recipes for non-alcoholic mixes, to giving a first cocktail party. Luckily my publishers were thinking along the same lines – and here is the book!

Michael Walker

A Classic Champagne Cocktail with orange Curaçao and brandy.

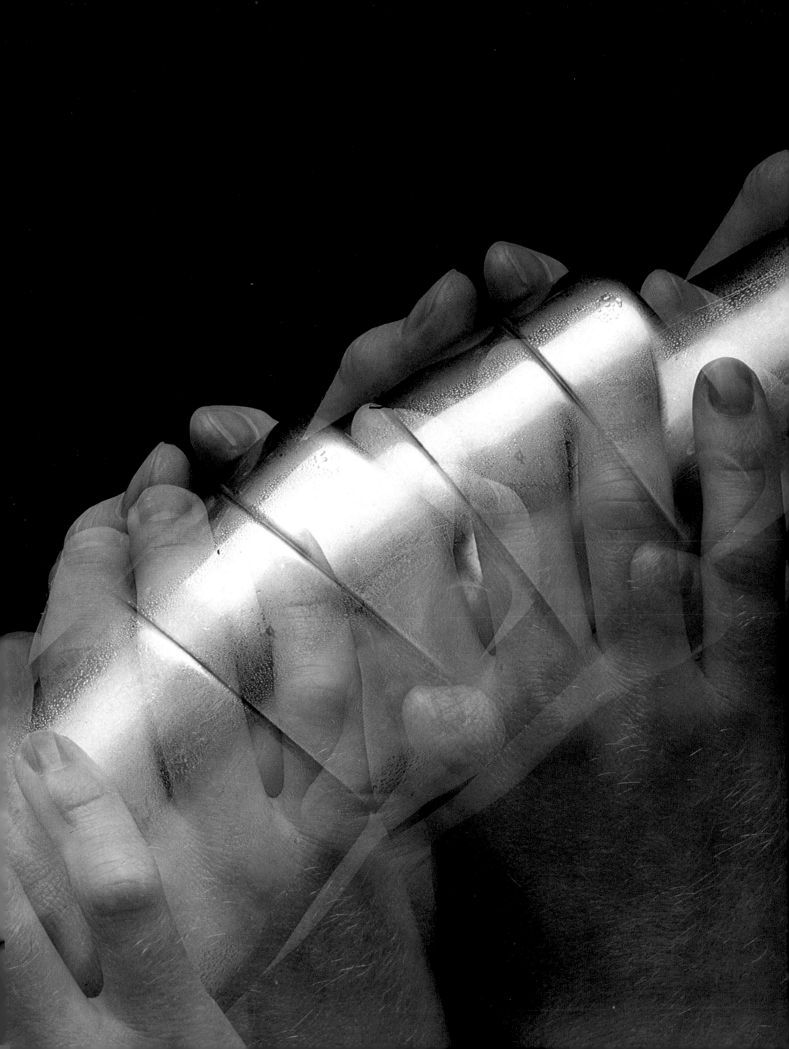

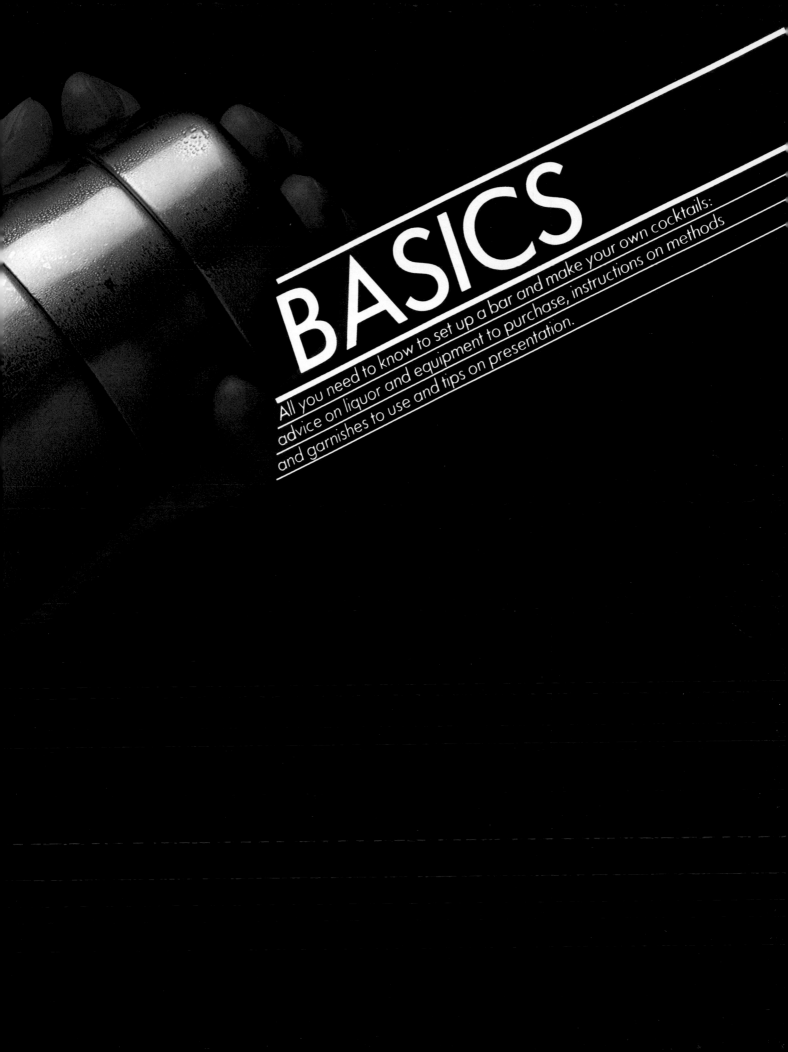

BASICS

All you need to know to set up a bar and make your own cocktails: advice on liquor and equipment to purchase, instructions on methods and garnishes to use and tips on presentation.

The Cocktail Story

Cocktails conjure up an atmosphere of the exotic – perhaps because they originated in the West Indies. But what exactly is a cocktail, what are its basic ingredients and how did it become popular outside its native home?

With the current upsurge of interest in cocktails today, many people are under the illusion that cocktails are an innovation of the twentieth century although, in fact, we have had cocktails with us from the reign of Elizabeth I. Origins of the word 'cocktail' are various: some say it comes from glasses decorated with cock's feathers, others from a wine cup called 'Coquetel'. The first mention of cocktails during the reign of Queen Elizabeth is from buccaneers who visited various ports along the coast of South America and the Caribbean. They were treated to concoctions of various liquors which had been distilled by an elementary process and then stirred with the root of a tree which resembled the tail of a bird indigenous to that part of the world. The spoon which is now used for stirring and muddling cocktails is in fact an evolution of this root. When the buccaneers returned to their home ports they introduced the mixed drinks that they had tasted on their travels and soon the idea of mixing drinks started to become popular.

Of course the early Elizabethans did not have the variety of spirits and wines that we have today and their types of mixed drinks became known as possett or cup, negus, mull or grog. A possett is generally a mixture of sugar, milk and spices curdled with hot milk, sometimes with the addition of eggs. A negus is a mixture of wines and spices which is heated with a little hot water; it is said that this was invented by a Colonel Negus in the reign of Queen Anne. A mull or mulled wine is know in other parts of Europe as *gluhwein*. It is made with wine, lemon and orange peel, sugar and spices.

Traditionally the ingredients were placed in a pewter tankard or pitcher and then a white hot poker immersed in the liquor. Nowadays the recommended method is to place the ingredients in a saucepan to heat! The recipe nearest to the traditional one used in Elizabethan times is the one for grog. The ingredients are dark rum, molasses or sugar, lemon juice and either hot water or tea. The method for making grog is similar to that of a negus.

From Elizabethan times to the early part of the twentieth century, the development of the cocktail was practically nil. But the advent of the twentieth century heralded a new cocktail era. Although the United States went through the period of Prohibition, abolished by President Roosevelt in 1929, many of the cocktails in existence today were invented then and became extremely popular. Following Prohibition came the Wall Street Crash and the Depression, but this did not daunt the more intrepid who were still able to obtain bottles of 'imported' booze in the eras of both Prohibition and Depression.

Although the present wave of enthusiasm over cocktails in Britain has come from the United States, the cocktail was in its heyday in Great Britain in the 1920s, with famous clubs such as The Embassy and hotels with cocktails bars such as the Savoy serving delicious blends to the 'smart set'. Then people began holding cocktail parties in their homes, but regrettably, due to World War II, the popularity of cocktails seemed to wane and in fact a resurgence of interest has only started in Britain during the last six years. However, in the United States the cocktail has always been an integral part of life with only a slight lull in popularity during the war years. Those were the days in the United States which brought about the advent of fruit Daquiris, Pinacoladas and other fruit-based cocktails which, like the original cocktails, came from the Caribbean.

With the accessibility of world travel today, more and more people are travelling to parts of the world that a few years ago were not easily reached. During these trips abroad, tourists are discovering new and exotic drinks made from indigenous fruits and liquors. On their return they try to find suppliers of the base ingredients of these drinks or bars which make them. In this way the popularity of exotic fruit cocktails has increased immensely over the last few years.

Nowadays a drinker will be far more discerning about mixed drinks. Whereas a few years ago a Martini could be any combination of gin and vermouth that the bartender cared to serve, the customer now will often specify the exact proportions of his cocktail and how it should be served, either 'on the rocks' or 'straight up',

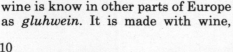

with a twist of lemon or an olive. The home bartender too has become much more than just an enthusiastic amateur and, with the ready availability of cocktail bar equipment and different liquors, woe betide the professional bartender who makes a slip in front of a well-versed amateur!

When setting up a bar at home, it is usually best not to be over-enthusiastic when purchasing liquor or equipment. A section of this book, 'Tricks of the Trade', deals with the few essentials you will need to start mixing a fair range of cocktails and how to extend your range of liquor and equipment slowly and inexpensively.

What is a Cocktail?

Every cocktail consists of the base, the modifier or aromatizer, and the colouring agent or special flavouring. The base is the predominant ingredient and the main ones are the spirits: gin, vodka, rum, brandy and whisky. With the more exotic cocktails you will find that there may be more than one aromatizer or flavouring agent and some have soda added as a finishing touch for a little effervescence.

The modifier acts as a smoothing agent, bringing out the flavour of the base. Modifiers are either Italian or French vermouth, wine, fruit juices, sugar, cream and eggs.

The colouring agent or special flavouring consists of the fruit syrups such as grenadine or orgeat, liqueurs and cordials. It is important to remember that flavouring agents must be used to flavour a cocktail delicately and not to remove the taste of the cocktail base; thus a rum-based cocktail will still have the flavour of the rum coming through and this will be enhanced by the modifier, flavouring agent and colourizer. Between the Sheets, for instance, is a rum-based cocktail with lemon juice as the modifier and Cointreau as the special flavouring. The flavour of the rum blends delicately with the lemon juice and Cointreau to produce a smooth effect.

It may be useful to know a little about the origins of the spirits you will be using as bases. It is not necessary to use the most expensive brands for mixing cocktails.

Gin comes from Holland and was first made by Franciscus de la Boe who was a professor of medicine at the University of Leiden. This distillation of juniper berries was originally sold in apothecary shops rather than the taverns, as it was used as medication for cleaning the blood. English soldiers brought the spirit back to England and during the reign of William of Orange the sales of gin escalated, leading to many private houses in London being turned into bars, or, as they were known then, 'gin shops'. Nowadays, there is a marked difference between English and Dutch gin: the English gin is quite smooth compared with the Dutch gin, which is heavily flavoured with juniper and now known as Genever. Although Genever can be bought in bottles, the best and oldest Genever is sold in stone crocks or crouchons.

The word 'vodka' immediately conjures up a picture of Russia, the land in which this fiery potion originated. The two countries which produce the best vodka today are Russia and Poland. Although vodka is supposed to be a tasteless spirit, there are several brands for sale which are flavoured with pepper, citrus fruits or even beef! Vodka was originally made from potato mash, but now nearly all vodka is made from pure grain such as rye, corn, or wheat. When gin is distilled, the second process after distillation is to add flavour, but with vodka the reverse happens. Vodka is processed by running it through charcoal until it is as clean and as tasteless as we know it. Vodkas do vary in quality and it is not always wise to buy the cheapest.

Of course, because of its lack of flavour, vodka is the most versatile of all the spirits, an ideal mixer for most cocktails. However, the Scandinavians, Russians and Poles have perfected the art of drinking vodka neat as an aperitif. Here the vodka is steeped in ice, poured into a chilled glass, then swallowed in one gulp. Usually a morsel of smoked sausage or fillet of herring is eaten with it.

Rum must rank as a very close second to vodka in its versatility as a base. Although rum does have a very distinctive flavour, it blends well with other liquors and is ideal for making fruit punches. Rum is produced in the West Indies and there are three main types: white, which is the Bacardi-type rum from Puerto Rico used in a Cuba Libre; light, which is the colour of whisky and is the base of most of the exotic cocktails; and dark, which has been, until recently, perhaps, the most popular rum in Britain.

Rum is a by-product of sugar and is made from the juice of sugar cane after it has been crushed. It is then reduced by boiling and what is left becomes a thick mixture, part of which turns into crystallized sugar and is removed. The remainder is known as molasses and is fermented and then distilled. Like

brandy and whisky, rum is aged in barrels, and the youngest rum exported for sale from the West Indies is usually about two to three years old. The older a rum gets, the smoother it becomes, and some rums over the age of fifteen years should be savoured neat as is a fine cognac or whisky. The proof spirit of rum varies between 70% and 151% (British) and every amateur bartender should endeavour to keep a small bottle of 151% proof in his stock to give a finishing touch to very special cocktails.

Brandy, which provides the finale to many a fine dinner, is made from the distillation of wine, and is in theory comparatively easy to produce. As wine boils at a lower temperature than water, brandy is made by simply allowing the vapour to evaporate, which leaves behind a basic form of brandy; when the vapour condenses it is known as eau de vie, 'water of life'. Cognac is the finest form of brandy and is produced in the area surrounding the town of Cognac. Cognac and brandy are both aged in casks and some are aged up to fifty years; the bottle labelled VSOP will be twenty to twenty-five years old. Another brandy

which is becoming increasingly popular is Armagnac; this comes from Gascony in France and has a more pungent bouquet than an ordinary Cognac. There are also brandies from Greece known as Metaxa, and from Peru called Pisco. Germany produces a brandy which is a little sweeter than the French brandies. California, which makes some fine wines, also produces brandy, but it is usually used in the making of cocktails only.

Of all the spirits, whisky presents the widest range of brands. The true Scotch was once the pure malt whisky of the Highlands. Now it has been adulterated by being blended with grain whiskies, although pure malts, such as Glenlivet, live on. If possible it is a good idea to have two brands of Scotch whisky in your bar: one for the mixing of cocktails and another brand, which has been mellowed in the cask for a while longer which gives it a smoother and more rounded taste, specially for the Scotch drinkers.

Then there is Irish whiskey which has a flavour of its own due to the additions of unmalted cereals in the still. It is, of course, essential in the making of Gaelic coffee.

From North America comes Canadian whisky, also with a distinctive taste which makes it impossible to confuse with any other type of whisky. It is made from a blend of corn and rye and is delicious served on the rocks with a dash of Angostura bitters and ginger ale. There are two American types of whiskey: Bourbon, which is made mainly of corn, and rye whiskey.

Whenever whisky is made, basically the same method is used. The grain is first made into a mash with water; water is of prime importance as it influences the flavour. Then malt and yeast are added in stages to turn it to alcohol. It is then vaporized and, when cooled, it becomes whisky. Before it is ready to be bottled it is aged in casks, sometimes up to twenty years. As with brandy, the older the whisky is, the better the flavour.

Methods

There are several different methods used in the making of cocktails, but the three basic ones are: blending the ingredients in an electric blender or liquidizer, stirring them in a mixing glass or the glass in which they are served, and shaking them in a cocktail shaker. Other methods, often used in conjunction with the basic ones, are floating, muddling and pouring.

Unless fruit or eggs are to be blended in the recipe, most cocktails can be either shaken or stirred. Shaking produces a colder drink and gives a cloudy appearance. A stirred cocktail remains clear and this is the method recommended for wine or vermouth cocktails, like a Martini or Manhattan, where the limpid look is greatly prized. There should be no confusion here, as all recipes specify the best way of making the cocktail.

It is of utmost importance that a cocktail be served cold. Shakers, mixing glasses and serving glasses can all be chilled in the refrigerator, at least an hour before use.

The order of putting ingredients in a shaker or mixing glass makes little difference to the drink itself, unless it is a colourfully layered Pousse Café. However, it is wise to put the cheaper ingredients in first in case you are interrupted in the middle of making the cocktail; the drink may have been spoilt, but you will not have wasted your expensive liqueurs or spirits.

Blending When a recipe includes fresh fruit or eggs, the cocktail must be blended. Blending also gives a frothy consistency which cannot be achieved by merely shaking the ingredients. The secret is not to blend for too long, otherwise the ice may turn to water and dilute the drink. When blending cocktails in an electric blender, it is essential to remember not to add soda or other highly effervescent ingredients before blending as you will probably end up with a rather messy explosion. When blending, air is being added to the cocktail and, although neither the alcoholic nor liquid content is being increased, the volume is. Ice is essential to a cocktail. Although cubed ice is acceptable for blending, cracked ice is far better. This not only saves wear and tear on the blades of the blender, but also preparation time.

Mixing or stirring This is done in a glass beaker, with the capacity of approximately 57cl (1 pint). The beaker should have a lip which is an aid for pouring; an ordinary household jug serves the purpose well. The ice used for stirring can be either cracked or cubed and, as always, should only be allowed to chill the cocktail and not dilute it. The drink should be stirred with a long mixing spoon. When stirring drinks with soda or other effervescent liquids, it is a good point to remember that if you stir the cocktail gently but briefly, the drink will hold its effervescence much longer than if it is briskly stirred. When the glass starts to perspire, the drink is ready for pouring.

Shaking Cocktails can be shaken with either cracked or cubed ice. Shake the ingredients briskly and pour as soon as the cocktail has been sufficiently chilled. You will know this when the shaker becomes cold and the

Shaking is one method of making a cocktail; for this you need a cocktail shaker. Here a Grasshopper is in the process of being made – a delicious cream cocktail with green crême de menthe.

15

Blending is essential for most of the exotic cocktails as a large number of them contain fruit. Fill the blender with crushed ice, pour in your fruit and liquors and switch on. Several seconds of blending will make you a smooth cocktail, full of flavour.

outside starts to sweat. The order of filling the shaker, as in any other method of preparing cocktails, is: first place the ice into the mixing equipment, then follow by the fruit juices, eggs or cream and lastly the liquor. Never use bad fruit or soured cream. When shaking your cocktail remember it is the cocktail and the shaker that is shaken and not you. There are various methods of shaking but, basically, the most comfortable position is the best. An easy and effective way of shaking the cocktail is to hold the shaker in front of you with your right hand firmly clasping the top of the shaker and the left hand supporting the base. The cocktail should then be shaken by using a brisk pumping action like that of a piston. Do not allow the cocktail to stand in the shaker with the ice as this will only lead to it being diluted.

Floating Sometimes a recipe calls for a high proof spirit to be floated on the top of a cocktail. Usually the spirit is poured over a spoon placed against the side of the glass as the cream would be on top of a liqueur coffee. Alternatively there is the Pousse Café which is a multi-coloured layered drink which can be made by pouring the heaviest liquor in first, then following it with the rest of the liquors, from the densest to the lightest, pouring them down the side of the glass. Or the liquors can be poured over an inverted spoon held in the glass. Otherwise just pour them into a glass and place it in the refrigerator; eventually the liquors will find their own levels, forming layers. When making Pousse Café it should be remembered that it is important to follow the recipe exactly and to pour the liquors into the glass in the order in which they are given. One recipe for Pousse Café is grenadine followed by Parfait d'amour and topped by maraschino.

Mixing completes the trio of main methods of making cocktails. Mixing a Manhattan means stirring a whisky of your choice (in this case, Irish) with sweet vermouth in a mixing glass with ice. What could be simpler!

Muddling The action of muddling is basically the way in which ingredients, such as the sugar and Angostura in an Old Fashioned and the sugar and mint in a Julep, are crushed with the heel of the mixing or muddling spoon, until they dissolve in the liquor.

Muddling and mixing are often used together, as, for example, in an Old Fashioned. In this, a sugar cube is placed in an old fashioned or rocks glass and three dashes of Angostura bitters and a measure of whisky are added. Then crush the sugar with the liquid until it dissolves: this is the action of muddling. Add two or three cubes of ice and cover with whisky and stir the drink again: this is mixing the drink. Finally, decorate with a maraschino cherry on a cocktail stick.

Pouring When drinks are served on the rocks, they are poured over ice. It is important to remember that a cocktail should never be poured higher than 6mm ($\frac{1}{4}$in) from the top of the glass. Wine should be poured so that the glass is only half full; in this way the bouquet can best be savoured. When adding decoration to a cocktail, always allow room for it so that the drink will not overflow.

Glasses and Garnishes

An attractive amber cocktail served in a glinting glass can make a drink even more appealing – especially when decorated with a slice of orange and a paper parasol … Here is a guide to glasses traditionally used for cocktails and how to garnish them.

There is a very wide range of glasses from which to make a selection, from the smallest cocktail glass to the largest goblet. The important thing to remember when buying glasses is to allow for generous measures of drink and room for garnishes, if desired. For a party, of course, glasses need not be purchased but can be hired from a local wine merchant, perhaps for free if you buy your liquor there.

With such a range it is essential to know which cocktail should be served in which glass; this depends on both appearance and the strength of the drink. The recipes tell you what, traditionally, is used for what, but, especially with the longer drinks, you can choose your own if you think it more attractive. Whichever glass you use, it is as well to note that iced drinks cause condensation on the glass, and if you don't want your furniture left with ring marks, provide coasters for yourself and your guests.

There are three glasses that you will need initially, and with these you can produce a good choice of cocktails, from a Martini to a Mai Tai. They are the cocktail glass, the old fashioned or whisky tumbler and the tall highball.

Classic cocktail These can vary in size from 5cl (2fl oz) to 28cl (10fl oz). A 28cl (10fl oz) Martini would be suicidal, so the average size glass recommended to start your stock of glasses would be 13cl (4½fl oz). Remember that the size of your glasses and measure should bear some relation as, if you are using a measure of 4cl (1½fl oz), then to use a glass which could not accommodate multiples of this would obviously not be viable. When working out measures it is important to remember that glasses should never be filled to the brim. Always make sure that you use real glass and not plastic, which taints the taste, nor glass covered with multi-

Above: left to right **Rocks glasses in two sizes, 23cl and 17cl (8fl oz and 6fl oz). Wine glass, 14cl (5fl oz). Cocktail glass 10cl (3½fl oz).**
Below: left to right **Fluted champagne glass 14cl (5fl oz). Tulip wine glass 17cl (6fl oz). Goblet 33cl (12fl oz). Cocktail glass 17cl (6fl oz).**

coloured designs, which detracts from the colour of the cocktail. Lastly, a cocktail glass should have a long stem; the purpose of this is to keep the cocktail chilled for as long as possible. If the bowl of the glass is held in a warm hand, the hand will become wet and the cocktail will lose its chill.

Highball or **Collins glass** These again vary in size from 14–45cl (5–16fl oz) and I recommend using a 23cl (8fl oz) or 28cl (10fl oz) glass. These glasses are usually straight sided, but there are some available with slightly flaring sides. Into the highball glass can go any drink from a straight lemonade, to a Mai Tai or even a beer.

Whisky tumbler This is also known as an old fashioned glass, rocks glass or Delmonico. This is similar in shape to a highball, but is usually about 11–14cl (4–5fl oz) and with flared sides. In these glasses you can serve fruit juices, sours or just plain drinks on the rocks.

Although these are the three basic glasses that you will need, there are of course many others, some of which will be mentioned here as well as some more unusual designs which you will discover are not in general usage, or you may find a particular glass that you may personally care for. But whatever glass you choose, remember that not only should a cocktail be pleasing to the palate, but it should also be pleasing to the eye, and this is where your choice of glass comes in.

If you are fortunate enough to possess a large freezer or refrigerator it is much nicer to chill your glasses before serving. This will not only help to keep the drink chilled a little longer, but a frosted glass is also extremely attractive to the eye. Another point to remember in connection with the presentation of glasses is cleanliness. When you have washed and rinsed your glasses in very hot water always use two clothes, one for drying and one, linen, for a final polish.

Other types of glasses which you can purchase are:

Champagne There are two types of champagne glass which are the champagne saucer and the champagne tulip which resembles a sherry glass, but which is twice the capacity. This smaller version could also be used for serving port or liqueurs.

Large goblet This is usually known as the Hoffman goblet, and is found in varying sizes from 23–62cl (8–22fl oz), although the size used most often is the 28cl (10fl oz). It was originally intended as a beer goblet, but lends itself perfectly to the more exotic cocktails as well.

Wine glasses There are so many types of wine glass that to list them all would take a book in itself. However what should be noted is that red wine is best served in a goblet of approximately 23cl (8fl oz), whereas white wine is best served in a smaller glass of approximately 17cl (6fl oz) which usually has a slightly longer stem than the red wine goblet.

Glass beer steins or **tankards** These can be used not only for beer but also for other drinks, such as Mint Juleps and Bloody Marys.

Pilsner This is another versatile glass and the most serviceable size to obtain is the 28cl (10fl oz). These glasses can be used for cocktails such as Pinacoladas or even to serve champagne after the glass and champagne have been well chilled in the refrigerator.

Brandy balloon or **brandy inhaler** The shape of this glass is unique and you may well decide to serve cocktails

in it which would certainly look most unusual. However, its shape is designed so that the brandy drinker may savour the full aroma of the brandy's bouquet. An interesting way in which to use this glass is to fill it with crushed ice and then make a Tequila Sunrise.

A final word on glass care: always make sure that your glasses are washed and put away after a party or a few drinks, as well as cleaning your bar or drinks cabinet and putting all the stock away. Note which stock should be replenished the following day. Always keep your bar well stocked not only with a good selection of liquor, but also of glasses and garnishes so that you can 'open up' at a moment's notice.

Garnishes
Nowadays there are more and more decorations appearing on the market for the cocktail bar, from miniature parasols made of paper to non-toxic fireworks which can make any cocktail party quite a sensation. Don't forget, however, that the most effective decorations can be made from the simplest of things, from a single pearl onion on a stick for a Gibson to several slices of tropical fruits for the more exotic cocktails. This is where your imagination can run riot and you can experiment with several combinations of decoration to delight your friends. A guide to the main garnishes for your bar is as follows:

Above: left to right **Tumbler 23cl (8fl oz)**. **Sherry glass 8.5cl (3fl oz)**. Below: left to right **Tumbler 45cl (16fl oz)**. **Highball 28cl (10fl oz)**. **Cocktail glass 11cl (4fl oz)**.

Maraschino cherries For really exotic garnishes you can now purchase cherries coloured yellow, green and blue as well as the usual red.

Olives (green) These should preferably be stuffed and are served with Dry Martinis.

Pearl onions To be served with a Gibson Martini.

Fresh fruit Lemon, orange and, if possible, limes, are important garnishes. Do avoid the canned or bottled fruit as the liquid in which they are preserved can taint a cocktail. Other fruits to use are pineapple, banana, mango, and peach.

Fresh mint This makes a delightful decoration to a cocktail and can be grown even in the smallest window boxes.

Castor (granulated) sugar Use it either as a sweetener for your drinks in place of sugar syrup or to frost the rims of cocktail glasses.

Fine salt Use to frost the rim of a Margarita glass.

Cocktail sticks These can either be made of wood or plastic, although the wooden sticks cannot be used more than once. The plastic ones are more decorative as they are coloured. If you intend to use the plastic sticks a second time, then they should be placed in boiling water to sterilize them.

Spices These can be sprinkled on the top of a cocktail, usually with cream. The most popular are cinnamon and grated nutmeg.

Vegetables Occasionally these can be used as a garnish, like celery in a Bloody Mary, or cucumber in a Cool Cucumber.

Straws Always have a good selection. The plastic ones are best; they are prettily patterned and some are flexible.

Essential Equipment

A shopping list for the beginner who wants to set up a cocktail bar – what you need for mixing, shaking and blending your drinks as well as for measuring 'jiggers', opening bottles and a host of other useful items.

Apart from glasses which have already been dealt with, the following equipment is necessary in setting up a bar if you wish to make cocktails as expertly as a professional bartender. Suggestions are also given on how to adapt kitchen equipment already in the home to your use. Suppliers of bar equipment for the licensed trade are to be found by looking in the classified section of the telephone directory. However, if there is no supplier within easy reach of you, then there is probably a local bar, hotel or restaurant which could either put you in touch with one or perhaps hire or even sell you some equipment of their own.

Cocktail shaker   There are several types of these and the most acceptable for the beginner is in two sections: one part is a plain glass beaker and the other half comprises a metal beaker which fits snugly over the rim of the glass one. The metal beaker has a pouring hole, often with a built-in strainer, and a cap. This is an extremely versatile piece of equipment as it makes an efficient shaker which is easy to clean, and the glass beaker can also be used as a mixing glass.

Hawthorne strainer   This is made

This is all the equipment you need for the main methods of making cocktails: shaking, blending and mixing. Left to right **A cocktail shaker, a blender with a Hawthorne strainer in front of it, a mixing glass with a long stirring spoon, and another type of cocktail shaker.**

of wire with perforations to allow the liquid of the cocktail to pass through without the ice falling into the glass. It has an edge of rolled wire to prevent spillage. There are other strainers on the market made of plated silver, but these should be avoided as they tend to taint the flavour of the cocktail if they become tarnished.

Mixing glass   This is a plain glass jug with a lip for pouring. It should have a capacity of approximately 84cl ($1\frac{1}{2}$ pints). Do not be tempted by fancy jugs of coloured glass or with patterns: the object of the mixing glass is to enable you to chill the cocktail as efficiently and as quickly as possible and to be able to see if any 'foreign body' has fallen in by mistake; this you can only spot through clear glass. In times of desperation a milk bottle can be used as both a mixing glass and shaker. The problem of sealing it for shaking is overcome by putting foil over the top and an elastic band fitted over the neck of the bottle to hold the foil in place.

Mixing spoon   This should have an oval bowl with a handle approximately 254mm (10in) long. It is best that the handle is not smooth as this may become slippery when wet: many are made with a spiral pattern on the handle.

Blender or **liquidizer**   This is the most expensive piece of equipment that you may have to purchase. Although it is possible to use a domestic food blender, it is far better to purchase a commercial blender which is equipped to cope with crushing ice, etc. When blending it is preferable to use cracked ice as this will save wear and tear on the blades and motor of your blender. A good blender should have several speeds or action settings and a resilient stainless steel or heavy duty plastic finish. The blending jar should be made of either stainless steel or heavy duty glass, with a detachable

27

Left to right **A knife and chopping board for slicing fruit, a squeezer for making juice, a bowl of sugar to sweeten cocktails, a nutmeg grater with nutmegs for garnishing, olives, Angostura bitters, a jug of cream, sugar lumps for a Classic Champagne Cocktail, a mixing glass, soda syphon and drinking straws.**

base containing the blades, which makes cleaning of the blades easy. It cannot be stressed enough that bar equipment must be kept scrupulously clean; the piece of equipment most likely to retain dirt is the area around the blades of a blender. To clean this, use a bottle brush which will prevent you cutting your fingers on the blades.

Ice equipment This consists of ice trays for the refrigerator and a well-insulated ice bucket with tongs. There are attachments to blenders which will also crush ice, but if you don't possess one, don't worry. Should you need to crush ice, wrap it in a clean tea towel and place it on a bread board or other hard surface; then hit it with a wooden mallet or meat tenderizer until the ice has been sufficiently cracked. Ice tongs or a large serving spoon for removing the ice from its bucket are also needed, but what you use is a matter of choice.

Wooden chopping board and knife These are used for cutting and preparing fruit for garnishing. The knife blade must always be kept sharp; more accidents occur when using blunt knives rather than sharp ones, because of too much pressure on the blade of a blunt knife when cutting.

Lemon squeezer Hopefully you will decide to use fresh fruit juices, and to make your own you will either need a blender attachment to extract the juice or a simple lemon squeezer. This is made of glass or heavy duty plastic and resembles a cone standing in a bowl which will catch all the juice. Although this method of juice extraction is laborious, the flavour of fresh fruit juices in a cocktail makes it all worthwhile.

Measure The standard measure is known as a jigger and holds 4cl (1½fl oz). Although measures are available in other sizes, this is the one most consistently used. If you do not have a measure, then remember that a standard liqueur glass is 2.8cl (1fl oz). However, anything can be used as a measure as long as it is consistently used throughout the recipe.

Bottle openers You can buy a combination of corkscrew, knife and bottle opener known as a waiter's friend, and it is exactly that. It resembles a scout knife and is a very useful piece of equipment.

Cloths You should have at least one for drying and one, preferably linen, for polishing your glasses before use. They should be kept both clean and dry.

Other items There are cocktail sticks, stirrers, straws, bowls for sugar and salt and fruit, nutmeg graters and a host of other items to add to your collection, which will make you the envy of your friends, and perhaps the professional bartender too.

Tricks of the Trade

A treasure trove of tips for the amateur barman: suggestions for a limited stock of liquor to produce a wide variety of cocktails, instructions for frosting glasses, how to make your own sugar syrup, and cures for that 'morning after' feeling.

When first starting a bar of your own, you will not be able to afford a complete range of liqueurs and spirits. Here is a guide as to what to buy to produce as many cocktails as possible from a relatively small selection of bottles.

Begin with the spirits that form the bases of most cocktails. The first to purchase is rum: either a bottle each of dark and white rum, or, if it is available, a bottle of light rum, which is whisky-coloured. Rum is the basis of many cocktails, from an Apricot Lady to a Zombie. In recipes which specify a measure of light rum, you can substitute half dark and half white rum.

The next purchase should be gin, used in cocktails from the Collins to the Martini. Then vodka, essential for the ever-popular Harvey Wallbanger. It is also good to 'spice up' a fruit punch, giving it quite a kick. Then brandy, the base for the delectable Brandy Alexander, or for use in Cobblers.

Ideally, your bar should have a range of whiskies comprising Scotch, Irish, Canadian, and Bourbon. However, this proves expensive, so for your first purchase buy Scotch, and then gradually build up your stocks.

Although there is a growing demand for tequila, it is not imperative to buy this at the initial stage, unless you are very keen on preparing Margaritas and Tequila Sunrises.

From the basic spirits, which could simply be mixed with sodas, move on to those liqueurs which are to be the most useful in the early stages. First Triple Sec or Cointreau: in mixing cocktails Triple Sec has proved more economical to use than Cointreau, although as a straight liqueur Cointreau has a smoother taste to it. Apricot Brandy or Apry is useful for making a range of cocktails from Apricot Sours to Mai Tais, when blended with rum and other liquors. Orange Curaçao is also a good liqueur for mixing; although it is not usually a base for cocktails, it can be added to many recipes, giving a rich orange taste.

White and dark crème de cacao are both invaluable as the popularity of the Alexander will testify. When white crème de cacao is mixed with green crème de menthe and cream, it makes the delightfully refreshing Grasshopper. Although the use of green crème de menthe is limited, it is delicious when served frappé, with a sprig of mint, at the end of a meal.

Galliano is another important purchase as, although it is not used in many cocktails, it is a necessary ingredient for the Harvey Wallbanger, which is ideal to serve at parties. The vodka and orange juice can be premixed, poured into jugs and refrigerated; when serving, just pour into highball glasses and top with Galliano. Galliano is also used in the creamy Golden Cadillac.

Lastly, there is Amaretto which, when mixed with an equal quantity of vodka, becomes a Godmother and, when mixed with an equal quantity of Scotch whisky, becomes a Godfather. It is also delightful when blended with strawberries and cream in a Julia. It is becoming more and more popular just drunk on its own or frappéed.

The two main non-alcoholic syrups required are grenadine, ideal for colouring, and orgeat which, like Amaretto, is almond-based. Orgeat is ideal when creating exotic cocktails of your own for, when mixed with rum and other liquors, it adds a certain mystique to the taste of the cocktail. Grenadine, on the other hand, although made from promegranates, is virtually tasteless and is ideal when

Necessary accessories: an ice bucket to hold the ice, with a shovel and tongs. Then, left to right, a corkscrew with a cork-brush, a measure, a dispenser top for bottles, and a chopping board and small sharp knife.

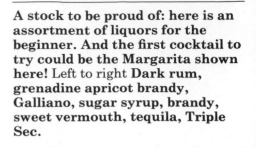

A stock to be proud of: here is an assortment of liquors for the beginner. And the first cocktail to try could be the Margarita shown here! Left to right **Dark rum, grenadine apricot brandy, Galliano, sugar syrup, brandy, sweet vermouth, tequila, Triple Sec.**

mixed with a little sugar to frost the rim of the glass to enhance the appearance of a cocktail. Syrups are inexpensive and can be obtained in many flavours from cerise to framboise and cassis. Sugar syrup is usually available, but it is not imperative to purchase it for your initial stock. You may even care to prepare your own from the following recipe: slowly bring to the boil equal parts of sugar and water, and simmer for one minute. Allow to cool, then pour into a bottle and store in a cool place.

Purchasing the right fruit juice is not always easy; although there are many brands available, finding the fruit juice which has the correct density is important to the appearance of the completed cocktail. When making a small number of cocktails, it is preferable to produce your own lemon juice and orange juice. However, if making cocktails for a large party, you may resort to canned or frozen juices. In this case it is worth paying a little extra for quality.

Angostura bitters, Worcestershire sauce and Tabasco sauce are also important; the former as an ingredient to enhance the flavour of many traditional and exotic cocktails, and the latter two in the production of the classic Bloody Mary and Virgin Mary, among others.

A sweet vermouth is another good bottle for the bar, especially if you want to make wine cocktails. Two delicious recipes are Apple Pie and Roman Holiday.

Tips and Hints

There are very few barmen who would willingly give away any of their secrets. Although we give you here a few hints for the preparation and finishing touches to your cocktails, it would take many years of trial and error to discover some of the tricks of skill used by bartenders.

The first and most important point is always keep your bar properly cleaned; this means not only making sure that all equipment is clean, but that the working surfaces and shelves are regularly wiped with a clean damp cloth.

When washing equipment by hand, whether glasses or cocktail shakers, use one bowl of water for washing and one for rinsing. If you have a lot of glasses to wash after a party, then change the water frequently and have the water as hot as you can bear. Drying and polishing cloths should

always be clean and dry. Even if they have been in a dishwasher, glasses should be polished with a dry linen cloth to make them gleam.

For decorating do not be afraid to use imaginative combinations of fruit and other garnishes to make the cocktail look enticing. Use unusual glasses in which to serve the cocktails and, if you're feeling extravagant, float orchids or roses in the larger ones.

An idea which always seems to impress is 'frosting' the rim of a glass with sugar, or with salt, as for a Margarita. When frosting with sugar, the best way of keeping the sugar firmly on the glass is as follows: dip the rim of the glass into the white of an egg, then dip lightly in castor (granulated) sugar. You may have to dip the glass into the sugar several times to achieve the desired effect, so don't be disappointed if you don't succeed the first time. For even greater effect, mix the castor (granulated) sugar with a little coloured syrup or vegetable dye. You will only need a few drops of the dye as the colour in these dyes is extremely strong and will stain clothes if spilt onto them. Using vegetable dyes for frosting can produce wonderful combinations of colour, but be warned! Only sweetened cocktails should have the rims frosted with sugar which will, of course, sweeten the cocktail even more when drunk.

When frosting a glass for a Margarita, take a wedge of lime or lemon and run it round the rim of the glass; hold the glass upside down to avoid the juice of the fruit from running down the stem. Then dip the glass gently into salt until the rim is evenly coated and voila! your glass is ready for the Margarita.

When a recipe calls for the addition of a 'twist' of either lemon or orange, this also means that a little of the oil or zest of the fruit as well as the actual peel should be added to the cocktail. To make a twist follow these simple instructions: take a piece of fresh fruit and cut an oval piece of peel approximately 25×3mm ($1 \times \frac{1}{8}$in). There must be no pith or meat of the fruit adhering to the twist. Holding it over the edge of the glass containing the cocktail, twist it between the thumb and forefinger. This will release a fine spray of oil or zest onto the surface of the drink, thereby giving it that professional touch.

Bar syrups are extremely useful

and it is a good idea to enlarge your collection of syrups as you progress with your bar expertise. Apart from the more common syrups, such as sugar or gomme, grenadine and orgeat, there are a host of others, such as menthe, cerise, fraise and framboise. These syrups are non-alcoholic and can be used to create exotically coloured and flavoured concoctions for any teetotal member of your party. If you run out of a liqueur such as crème de cassis when making a Kir, it would be hardly noticeable if you substituted cassis syrup. Many barmen prefer to use sugar syrup in cocktails rather than sugar, as sugar takes time to dissolve.

Every once in a while you will need to go through the stock in your bar and sort out all those bottles which have been left with the odd half measure, or bottles of liqueurs or syrups that are beginning to crystallize. Here is your chance to experiment. Depending on how much liquor you wish to write off, invite a couple of friends over and, with what you have left, start inventing your own concoctions. This is where you score over the professional bartender who, day after day, has to churn out a steady routine of run-of-the-mill cocktails.

There are obvious dangers in this form of experimenting, so here are a few 'hair of the dog' recipes. Although, from a medical point of view, adding alcohol to a body already totally overindulged will not do the slightest bit of good, the effect it produces will probably help you over the worst of 'the morning after'.

If you know that you are in for a night on the town, do try to line your stomach with either a pint of milk or some olive oil which should cushion the effect of the alcoholic onslaught. And when you've staggered home, try to drink at least 114cl (2 pints) of water or a glass of water with 2 teaspoons of liver salts before collapsing. Remember that alcohol dehydrates the system, which contributes to a hangover, so the more liquid that you drink – non-alcoholic, of course – before you retire, the better you will feel the next morning.

For morning afters, a good standby that should be part of any bar is Fernet Branca. Either take a liqueur glass neat or add soda to 1 measure and drink it straight back. It should start taking effect after 10–15 minutes. Other useful recipes are:

Bar syrups, such as sugar and strawberry, are extremely useful for flavouring or colouring. To present drinks prettily, frost the glass first, just as the Princess Margaret, a non-alcoholic cocktail, is shown served here. Tabasco sauce gives a sharpness to the Prairie Oyster being prepared here – it's a cure for that 'morning after' feeling. Always chill glasses before serving, like the cocktail glass on the right, garnished with an olive and ready for a Martini.

Prairie Oyster I

1 egg yolk
Cayenne pepper
1 dash Worcestershire sauce
1 dash Tabasco
1 teaspoon wine vinegar
1 measure brandy

Mix the ingredients very carefully in a rocks glass, ensuring that you do not break the yolk. Drink in one gulp. For Prairie Oyster II, see 'Non-alcoholic Cocktails'.

Savoy Corpse Reviver

1 measure brandy
1 measure Fernet Branca
1 measure white crème de menthe

Shake ingredients well with ice and strain into a cocktail glass.

Morning Fizz

1 measure whisky
½ egg white
1 dash lemon juice
2 dashes sugar syrup
¼ measure Pernod

Shake ingredients well with ice and pour into a highball glass. Top with soda.

Harry Wallbanger

1 measure vodka
1 measure Cointreau
2 measures orange juice
1 measure orange squash (orangeade)

Shake ingredients well with ice and pour into a large goblet. Top up with champagne.

Cinzano Saver

1 measure rye whiskey
1 measure Cinzano rosso
2 dashes Angostura bitters
2 dashes lemon juice
2 dashes Tabasco

Shake ingredients well with ice and pour into a rocks glass. Decorate with a slice of lemon.

A last thought for those who do not have the patience nor the interest, or perhaps lack confidence in mixing drinks: they can make bartending extremely easy for themselves. There are mixes available in liquid or powder form for many of the well-known cocktails, such as a Collins or a Pinacolada. All you need to do is add your favourite base liquor, mix, and there is your cocktail! Unfortunately, most of the brands available at present cannot compete with a cocktail made with fresh ingredients. And then, surely there is nothing more fulfilling than to make your own cocktails for yourself and your friends.

Glossary

There is no need to feel at a loss with any of the terms in this book. Here is a list of all the liquors, familiar and unfamiliar, which appear in the recipes, plus explanations of Sours, Flips and other drink-types.

Advocaat
A liqueur originally produced in Holland, made from egg yolks, sugar and spirits.

Almond syrup
Non-alcoholic flavouring known as orgeat.

Angostura bitters
A rum base with the addition of herbs, produced only in Port of Spain, Trinidad.

Applejack
An American version of Calvados, but lacking the subtlety of the French variety.

Apry
Another name for Apricot liqueur.

Banane (crème de)
A banana-flavoured liqueur.

Benedictine
A liqueur made from herbs, roots and sugar with a Cognac base. Made by the Benedictine monks.

Bitters
See Angostura, although there are other brands and flavours, including orange.

Bourbon
An American whiskey made from grain, which is at least 51% corn, and aged in charred oak barrels.

Brandy
Primarily a distillation from grapes, aged for three years. Generally, a distillation from fruit.

Cacao (crème de)
Chocolate and vanilla-flavoured liqueur, available in dark brown or white.

Calvados
A French apple brandy; the best produced is from Normandy. It is best consumed after ageing for ten years.

Campari
A bitter Italian red aperitif, usually taken with soda and decorated with a twist of orange.

Cassis
Blackcurrant flavour, either a non-alcoholic syrup or an alcoholic liqueur called crème de cassis.

Champagne
A light sparkling wine, usually white, from the Champagne district of France.

Chartreuse
A green or yellow liqueur made by the Carthusian monks. The former is said to contain 130 different herbs.

Cider
Fermented apple juice.

Cinzano
The brand name of a popular variety of vermouths.

Cognac
Brandy from the Cognac region of France around the Charente river.

Cointreau
A distinctive clear liqueur made from oranges.

Collins
A mixture of a base liquor, lemon juice and soda.

Curaçao
A liqueur made in the West Indies from the peel of dried green oranges. It is usually orange, but can be green, blue or white.

Drambuie
A very old Scots liqueur, made from whisky, heather, honey and herbs.

Dubonnet
A popular French aperitif with a quinine flavour, available in red or white.

Fernet Branca
A bitters of Italian origin.

Flip
A drink made with eggs.

Fraise
Available as a non-alcoholic syrup or as a liqueur called crème de fraise, made from strawberries.

Framboise
Available as a non-alcoholic syrup or a liqueur called crème de framboise, made from raspberries.

Frappé
To serve a cocktail over finely crushed ice.

Frost
Either to chill a glass or edge the rim with sugar or salt.

Galliano
A sweet Italian liqueur, yellow in colour, made from vanilla.

Gin
A distillation of grain with a flavouring of juniper.

Gomme
A syrup made from sugar.

Grand Marnier
A French liqueur made from oranges.

Grenadine
A red non-alcoholic syrup made from pomegranates.

Highball
A tall cylindrical glass usually about 28cl (10fl oz). Also a drink, usually 2 measures of a base liquor topped with ice and a soda or mixer, but not citrus juices.

36

Kahlua
A coffee liqueur from Mexico.

Kirsch
A white brandy made from cherry pits.

Kummel
A colourless liqueur flavoured with caraway.

Maraschino
A liqueur made from black cherries.

Menthe (crème de)
A mint-flavoured liqueur, either white or green.

Metaxa
Greek brandy.

Mulls
A hot wine punch, originally kept warm by putting a white hot poker into the drinking receptacle.

Noyaux (crème de)
An almond-flavoured liqueur, pink in colour, made from the stones of various fruits.

Orgeat
A non-alcoholic syrup flavoured with almonds.

Ouzo
A Greek anise-flavoured aperitif.

Parfait d'amour
A violet-coloured liqueur, scented and spiced.

Pastis
A French anise-flavoured liqueur.

Pernod
An anise-flavoured Pastis, similar in taste to the Greek ouzo.

Port
Made in the same way as sherry, but vintage port is from a particularly good year and is stored in wooden casks for at least two years before bottling. White port is also available, but lacks the body of a ruby or tawny. Classic years are 1927, 1935, 1942, 1947, 1950, 1955 and 1960.

Pousse Café
A liqueur of anisette, Curaçao and cacao. Also a cocktail in which various liqueurs of different densities are layered.

Punch
A drink of mixed spirits or wines with the addition of spices, fruit juices and sugar. Can be served either hot or cold.

Punt e Mes
A dark and bitter Italian aperitif.

Rum
A distillation of molasses from crushed sugar cane. The colour can vary from white rum to dark. Chiefly produced in the West Indies.

Rye
A Canadian whiskey made with at least 51% rye and matured in oak barrels.

Sambuca
An anise-flavoured Italian liqueur, usually served with two coffee beans floating on the top.

Sherry
A fortified wine where the fermentation has been arrested and brandy added to the liquor. Produced chiefly in Spain and Portugal, although Californian sherry and port is produced, but the quality is doubtful. Available as dry (fino), medium (amontillado) and sweet (oloroso).

Sour
A cocktail consisting of a base (usually brandy or whisky), a flavouring (a fruit brandy or liqueur) and lemon juice, shaken with a little sugar and ice. Can be served on the rocks or straight up.

Southern Comfort
A liqueur of American origin with a whiskey base and flavoured with peaches.

Strega
A yellow Italian liqueur made from many fruits and herbs.

Tequila
A colourless spirit made from the fermented juice of a cactus plant from Mexico. The plant is known as the agave, American aloe, maguey or mescal.

Tia Maria
A Jamaican coffee liqueur.

Toddies
A mixture of spirit and hot water.

Triple Sec
An orange-flavoured liqueur from the West Indies, similar to Cointreau.

Vermouth
A wine fortified with herbs.

Vodka
Usually a colourless and practically tasteless distillation of grain.

Wine
Usually the fermented juice of grapes, but also a liquor made from other fruits by fermentation.

Whisk(e)y
A distillation of grain, malt, sugar and yeast.

RECIPES

Included are the well-known Martini and Manhattan; the exotic Mai Tai; dreamy cream concoctions; champagne cocktails for indulgence; and 'mocktails' for the teetotaller.

Traditional Cocktails

Popular aperitifs, like Martinis and Manhattans and their variations, the well-known Harvey Wallbanger, the traditional drink of the South – Mint Julep – and a wealth of lesser-known but equally enticing cocktails: all appear here with simple instructions.

Here are 60 step-by-step recipes for traditional cocktails known by bartenders and cocktail enthusiasts worldwide – cocktails from the Americano to the Za-Za.

The recipe section begins with traditional cocktails and goes on to exotic, cream and wine concoctions ending with non-alcoholic cocktails. The word 'traditional' may therefore be a little ambiguous. Here it means the popular cocktails which do not include fresh fruit or cream in the recipe; these appear in their relevant sections.

There are variations on several of the cocktails; a Manhattan, for instance, becomes a Dry Manhattan when dry vermouth is substituted for sweet. Or a Bronx becomes a Silver Bronx with the addition of an egg white. Recipes for the basic traditional cocktails are all given, with some of their variations.

The measure referred to in the recipes is a jigger or 4cl (1½fl oz), but anything may be used as long as the measure remains consistent throughout the recipe. A dash is a very small quantity, about ⅛ teaspoon.

Probably the most popular aperitifs today are based on vermouths which are mixtures of wines and sometimes as many as 40 different herbs, spices and roots.

The main spirits used as bases in the making of cocktails are gin, whisky, vodka, rum and brandy. These five spirits vary according to the country in which they are produced; the flavour of Irish whiskey, for instance, is different from Scotch. Gin ranges from the original Dutch gin or Genever, made with juniper berries, to the English dry gin, which was first brought to England in the late seventeenth century. Although vodka is supposed to be tasteless, every bartender has his own favourite brand, and there are also available flavoured vodkas such as lemon, mint and even pepper!

There are basically three different types of rum: white, light (which is the colour of whisky) and dark. In any recipe shown using rum, the type will be clearly shown to avoid confusion. Most rum-based cocktails, however, are to be found in 'Exotic Cocktails'.

Last but not least is brandy. Brandy is produced in any country where grapes are grown; and it should be remembered that true Cognac only comes from the town of Cognac in France, which is an area either side of the Gironde and Charente rivers. There is another form of brandy made from apples known in America as Applejack, and a more refined version produced in Europe known as Calvados.

Once you have become confident in mixing drinks, you may wish to invent a cocktail of your own. Do not try out too many at once – the majority of cocktails were not designed to be consumed in quantity! You should also avoid drinking cocktails whose base spirit differs; for example, don't switch from a Dry Martini to a Manhattan to a Sidecar, thereby mixing gin, whisky and brandy. When experimenting mix one cocktail each evening. Trying new cocktails helps you to learn recipes and advise others as to what *they* should choose for their aperitifs.

Left to right **Black Russian (recipe page 43), Americano, Alpine Glow, Après Ski.**

Adonis

1 measure sweet vermouth
2 measures dry sherry
2 dashes Angostura bitters

Place 3–4 ice cubes into a mixing glass, then pour in the ingredients. Stir quickly, allowing the cocktail to chill without the ice melting. Strain into a cocktail glass and decorate with a twist of orange peel.

Alpine Glow

1 measure Cointreau or Triple Sec
2 measures lemon juice
4 measures brandy
4 measures dark rum
2 dashes grenadine

Place 3–4 ice cubes into the shaker, then pour in the ingredients. Shake vigorously and pour ice and liquor into a highball glass or small tankard. Decorate the glass with a slice of lemon, sprig of mint (if available), a cocktail cherry and two straws. Obviously, from the name of the cocktail and its ingredients, you can see that it will definitely keep out the winter's chill – but not to be taken before attempting the slopes!

Americano

1 measure Campari
1 measure sweet vermouth
Soda to top up, optional

Stir the ingredients well with ice in a
mixing glass and strain into a cocktail
glass. Decorate with either a twist of
lemon or orange, according to taste.
Alternatively, the liquor and ice can
be poured into a highball or rocks
glass and topped with soda.

Après Ski

1 measure green crême de menthe
1 measure Pernod
1 measure vodka
Lemonade to top up

Shake the ingredients well with ice
and pour into a highball glass and top
with lemonade. Decorate with 2 thin
straws, a slice of lemon and a sprig of
fresh mint.

Left to right **Embassy Royal (recipe page 44), The Classic, Collins, Freddy Fudpucker and Sherry Flip (both recipes page 44).**

Between the Sheets

1 measure rum
1 measure brandy
1 measure Cointreau or Triple Sec
1 measure lemon juice

Shake the ingredients well with ice, then strain into a cocktail glass. This is an exciting variation on the Sidecar, originally invented in the West Indies.

Black Russian

2 measures vodka
1 measure Kahlua or Tia Maria
Coca-Cola to top up, optional

Fill a rocks glass with ice and then add the ingredients and stir.
Another variation on the Black Russian is to make it in a highball glass and top with Coca-Cola. For a White Russian, see 'Cream Cocktails'.

Bloody Mary

1 measure vodka
3 measures tomato juice
1 dash Worcestershire sauce
1 dash Tabasco sauce
1 dash lemon juice

Half fill a mixing glass with ice and add black pepper, salt, Worcestershire sauce, Tabasco sauce, lemon juice and celery salt. Then put in the vodka and tomato juice. Stir well and pour into a highball glass or goblet. Decorate with a stick of celery or 1 thick straw.

Blue Blazer

2 measures Irish whiskey
1 measure clear honey
½ measure lemon juice
2–3 measures water

Place the ingredients in a saucepan and slowly bring to the boil, or heat until the honey has dissolved completely. Pour into a rocks glass with a teaspoon in it (this prevents the glass cracking if the liquor is too hot).
This is not only an extremely warming drink during the winter months, but is also a remedy for colds and influenza. It may not get rid of your cold completely, but it certainly makes it a little more bearable!

Bronx

1 measure gin
½ measure dry vermouth
½ measure sweet vermouth
½ measure orange juice

Shake well with ice and strain into a cocktail glass. Decorate with a slice of orange.
A Bronx cocktail may also be made by omitting the sweet vermouth and doubling the quantity of dry vermouth.

Bullshot

Another variation of the Bloody Mary, but use consommé instead of tomato juice.

Both Bloody Mary and Bullshot are delightful for a weekend brunch and can be guaranteed to chase away hangovers.

The Classic

1 measure brandy
¼ measure lemon juice
¼ measure maraschino
1 measure orange Curaçao

Shake ingredients well with ice and strain into a chilled cocktail glass. Decorate with a maraschino cherry on a cocktail stick.

COBBLERS

Most spirits and wines can be used as a base for a Cobbler, which is a delightfully refreshing iced and sweetened long drink. A Cobbler is usually made in a 28–33cl (10–12fl oz) glass. Here are two variations.

Cherry Cobbler

1 measure gin
½ measure cherry brandy
¼ measure lemon juice
2 dashes sugar syrup or
1 teaspoon sugar

Fill a glass with crushed ice, and add all the ingredients. Stir well until the drink is blended and the sugar has dissolved. If desired, top with more ice and decorate with a slice of lemon, a maraschino cherry and 2 thin straws.

Wine Cobbler

4 measures wine
¼ measure lemon juice
¼ measure orange juice
1 measure orange Curaçao
1 dash soda

Prepare and present as for a Cherry Cobbler, but substitute a slice of orange for lemon.

Collins

This is the recipe for a traditional Tom or John Collins; however, other spirits may be substituted for gin.

1 measure gin
Juice of 1 lemon
1 teaspoon sugar
1 dash Angostura bitters
Soda to top up

Into a highball glass put all the ingredients. Stir until the sugar has dissolved and then top with soda. Stir again and decorate with a slice of lemon and two thin straws.

Depth Charge

1 measure brandy
1 measure Calvados
¼ measure grenadine
¾ measure lemon juice

Shake ingredients well with ice. Strain into a cocktail glass with a twist of lemon.
An ideal shock to the system for that morning after the night before!

East India

1 measure orange Curaçao
2 measures pineapple juice
2 measures brandy
2 dashes Angostura bitters
Soda to top up

Shake ingredients well with ice. Pour into a highball glass and top with soda. Decorate with a slice of lemon, 2 thin straws and a maraschino cherry.

Embassy Royal

1 measure Bourbon whiskey
1 measure Drambuie
1 measure sweet vermouth
2 dashes orange juice

Shake ingredients well with ice. Strain into a cocktail glass and decorate with a twist of orange.

FLIPS

A flip is made with any base liquor shaken with an egg. The most popular of all the Flips is the one made with sherry, and so this is the recipe given.

Sherry Flip

1 egg
1 glass cream sherry

Place six cubes of ice into a blender with one egg and the glass of sherry. Blend until smooth and creamy and pour into a goblet. Sprinkle the top of the drink with grated nutmeg.

Fort Lauderdale

1 measure light rum
½ measure sweet vermouth
¼ measure orange juice
¼ measure lime juice

Shake ingredients well with ice and pour into a rocks glass. Decorate with a slice of orange and a cherry.

Foxhound

1 measure brandy
½ measure cranberry juice
¼ measure kummel
1 dash lemon juice

Shake ingredients well with ice and pour into a rocks glass. Decorate with a slice of lemon.
This traditional English cocktail is usually served before game during the shooting season.

Freddy Fudpucker

1 measure tequila
Galliano
Orange juice

Fill a highball glass with ice and add the tequila. Fill to within 12mm (½in) of the top of the glass with orange and float the top of the drink with Galliano. Decorate with a slice of orange and 2 thin straws.
As many of you will recognize, this is yet another variation on the Harvey Wallbanger.

Gloom Chaser

1 measure Grand Marnier
1 measure orange Curaçao
1 measure lemon juice
1 dash grenadine

Shake ingredients well with ice. Then strain into a cocktail glass with a twist of orange.
Another cocktail with a similar name, but not to be confused with it, is the Gloom Raiser.

Gloom Raiser

2 measures gin
¾ measure dry vermouth
2 dashes Pernod
2 dashes grenadine

Place into a mixing glass with ice cubes and stir well. Strain and serve into a cocktail glass with a maraschino cherry.

Golden Tang

4 measures vodka
2 measures Strega
1 measure crème de banane
1 measure orange juice

Shake ingredients well with ice and pour into a highball glass.

There is a tale that this was originally invented by a travel guide to cure, not only her own ailments, but also those of her clients. There is as yet no record of success or failure.

Harvard

1 measure gin
¾ measure dry vermouth
2 dashes Pernod
2 dashes grenadine

Place into a mixing glass with ice, stir well and strain into a cocktail glass.
In the United States all the best universities have their own cocktail. Perhaps someone in Britain will one day invent an Oxford or Cambridge . . .

Harvey Wallbanger

1 measure vodka
Galliano
Orange juice

Fill a highball glass with ice and add vodka. Pour in orange juice to within 12mm (½in) of the top of the glass. Float the top of the drink with Galliano. Decorate with a slice of orange and 2 straws.

Inca

1 measure gin
1 measure sweet vermouth
1 measure dry vermouth
1 measure dry sherry
1 dash orgeat syrup
1 dash Angostura bitters

Stir ingredients well with ice in a mixing glass. Pour into a rocks glass and decorate with half a slice of pineapple and a maraschino cherry.

Jade

1 measure light rum
½ measure green crème de menthe
½ measure orange Curaçao
½ measure lime juice

Shake ingredients well with ice and strain into a cocktail glass. Decorate with a slice of fresh lime.
This cocktail can also be served as a long drink on the rocks, topped with soda in a highball glass.

Left to right **Gloom Raiser, Jade, Katinka (recipe page 46), Foxhound.**

Katinka

1 measure apricot brandy
1½ measures vodka
½ measure lime juice

Shake ingredients well and serve over crushed ice in a cocktail glass. Decorate with a sprig of mint.

MANHATTANS

No cocktail book would be complete without the Manhattan or the Martini and this is no exception. We have also included 2 variations on the original theme.

Manhattan

2 measures rye whiskey
1 measure sweet vermouth
1 dash Angostura bitters

This can be served with or without ice, but should always be made in the mixing glass with ice. Stir, and either serve in a rocks glass with ice, or strain into a cocktail glass. Decorate with a maraschino cherry.

Dry Manhattan

Make as a Manhattan, using the same ingredients, but substituting dry vermouth for sweet vermouth. A twist of lemon or an olive may be substituted for a cherry.

Perfect Manhattan

1 measure rye whiskey
1 measure dry vermouth
1 measure sweet vermouth
1 dash Angostura bitters

Make as a Manhattan.

MARTINIS

Surely the most well known of all cocktails and yet probably the most abused, for although making a Martini is simple, it still needs care. Martinis, of course, can be served straight up or on the rocks according to taste. The classic Martini is based on gin, but you can make a Vodka Martini or Vodkatini, popularized in recent years by James Bond – or even a Tequila Martini.

Martini

3 measures gin
1 drop dry vermouth

Place 4–6 ice cubes into your mixing glass and add the gin and vermouth. Stir the liquor carefully, and before the ice starts to melt, strain into a chilled cocktail glass. Serve garnished with either a twist of lemon or an olive.

Gibson Martini

Another variation made in exactly the same way as a classic Martini, but garnished with a pearl onion.

Mint Julep

2 measures Bourbon whiskey
1 teaspoon sugar
Sprig of mint
Soda

In a highball glass, put the sugar, mint and a little soda. Mash these together well. Then add the Bourbon and top with soda or plain water.

Martini Gibson – the famous traditional cocktail garnished with a single pearl onion. The shape of the elegant cocktail glass in which it is served is now automatically associated with a Martini.

Negroni

1 measure Campari
1 measure gin
1 measure sweet vermouth

Stir ingredients well in a mixing glass with ice. This drink can either be strained and served straight up with a twist of orange, or served on the rocks with a slice of orange and a splash of soda.

Olympic

1 measure brandy
1 measure orange juice
1 measure orange Curaçao

Shake ingredients well with ice and strain into a cocktail glass with a twist of orange.

Oracabessa

1 measure crême de banane
½ measure lemon juice
1 measure dark rum
½ sliced banana
Lemonade to top up

Shake the liqueur, lemon juice and rum with ice and pour into a highball glass. Place the sliced banana on top of liquor and then top with lemonade. Decorate with 2 thin straws, sliced pineapple or banana and a maraschino cherry.

Left to right **Sidecar, Singapore Sling, Stinger** (recipe page 51), **Rusty Nail, Shanghai Gin Fizz.**

Orange Blossom

1 measure apricot brandy
½ measure Galliano
½ measure orange juice
1 measure vodka
Ginger ale to top up

Shake ingredients well with ice and pour into highball glass; top with ginger ale. Decorate with a slice of orange, a maraschino cherry and 2 thin straws.

Pink Almond

½ measure crême de noyaux
½ measure orgeat
1 measure whisky
½ measure lemon juice
½ measure kirsch

Shake ingredients well with ice and pour into a rocks glass. Decorate with a slice of lemon.

Polonaise

1 measure brandy
½ measure dark rum
½ measure lemon juice
½ measure grenadine
½ measure dry sherry
2 dashes Angostura bitters

Shake ingredients well with ice and strain into a cocktail glass. The liquor can also be poured straight into a rocks glass. Decorate with a twist of lemon.

Polynesia

1 measure light rum
1 measure passion fruit juice
¼ measure lime juice
1 egg white

Place all the ingredients with ice in a blender for 10 seconds and then pour into a cold champagne saucer. Decorate with a slice of fresh lime and a cherry.

Pompano

1 measure gin
½ measure dry vermouth
1 measure grapefruit juice
3 dashes orange bitters

Shake ingredients well with ice and then pour into a rocks glass. Decorate with a slice of orange and 2 small straws.

Prince Edward

1 measure Scotch whisky
½ measure dry vermouth
¼ measure Drambuie
Soda to top up

Shake ingredients well with ice and then pour into a rocks glass. Top with soda. Garnish with a slice of orange and a maraschino cherry.

Rhett Butler

1 measure orange Curaçao
½ measure lime juice
½ measure lemon juice
1 measure Southern Comfort
Soda to top up

Shake ingredients well and strain over crushed ice in a highball glass. Top with soda. Garnish with a slice of orange and a sprig of fresh mint with 2 thin straws.

Rob Roy

Many an amateur barman has been caught out with a Rob Roy because it is not well known. This is made in just the same way as a Manhattan, but Scotch is used instead of rye whiskey.

2 measures Scotch whisky
1 measure sweet vermouth
1 dash Angostura bitters

Stir the liquor in a mixing glass with ice. Either pour it straight into a rocks glass, or strain into a cocktail glass and serve. Decorate with a maraschino cherry.

Rosé Glow

½ measure gin
¼ measure Campari
¼ measure Cinzano rosé
¼ measure Cinzano bitters
¼ measure Cointreau or Triple Sec
½ measure apricot juice

Shake ingredients well with ice. Then strain into a cocktail glass and garnish with a maraschino cherry.

Rusty Nail

An all-time favourite with Scotch drinkers.

1 measure Scotch whisky
1 measure Drambuie

Pour into a mixing glass with ice and stir. Then either strain into a cocktail glass and serve, or strain into a rocks glass over crushed ice or pour straight into a rocks glass.

Shanghai Gin Fizz

½ measure gin
½ measure yellow Chartreuse
½ measure Benedictine
½ measure lemon juice
Soda to top up

The ingredients should be shaken well with ice and poured into a highball glass. Then top with soda. Decorate with a slice of lemon, a maraschino cherry and 2 thin straws.

Sidecar

1 measure brandy
1 measure Cointreau or Triple Sec
1 measure lemon juice

Shake ingredients well with ice, then strain into a cocktail glass. Garnish with a twist of lemon.

Singapore Sling

1 measure gin
1 measure cherry brandy
1 measure lemon juice
1 teaspoon sugar
Soda to top up

Shake ingredients well with ice. Then pour contents into a highball glass and top with soda. Decorate with a slice of lemon and a maraschino cherry with 2 thin straws.

SOURS

Any spirit can be turned into a sour by shaking it with lemon juice and sugar or sugar syrup.

Whisky Sour

2 measures Scotch or Bourbon
1 measure lemon juice
½ teaspoon sugar

Shake well with ice and pour into a rocks glass. Decorate with a slice of orange, speared with a cherry. Alternatively, add ½ egg white and shake with the ingredients. This will make the cocktail light and frothy.

Fruit Sour

1 measure Scotch or Bourbon
1 measure fruit liqueur of choice
1 measure lemon juice

Make as a Whisky Sour. The sugar has been left out of the ingredients as the fruit liqueur is sweet enough on its own.
Sours are generally served on the rocks and decorated with a slice of orange, a maraschino cherry and 2 short thin straws.

STINGERS

Stingers can be made with any liquor providing it is in equal parts with white crème de menthe.

Classic Stinger

1 measure brandy
1 measure white crème de menthe

Shake these ingredients well with ice. Then strain the liquor into a cocktail glass over crushed ice.

Tall Dutch

1 measure Advocaat
1 measure light rum
½ measure dark rum
1 measure orange juice
14cl (¼ pint or ⅔ cup US) milk
1 teaspoon sugar
2 pinches ground cinnamon

Place ingredients with 6 ice cubes into a blender and blend for 10 seconds. Pour into a highball glass or tumbler and sprinkle with nutmeg.

Toronto

Yet again, another one for the morning after . . .

2 dashes sugar syrup or
1 teaspoon sugar
1 measure Fernet Branca
2 measures rye whiskey
1 dash Angostura bitters

Stir ingredients well with ice in a mixing glass. Pour into a rocks glass and decorate with a slice of orange.

Trinity

1 measure rye whiskey
1 measure dry vermouth
1 dash orange bitters
1 dash white crème de menthe

Shake ingredients well with ice, then strain into a cocktail glass with a twist of lemon.
A Trinity can sometimes be varied by adding a dash of lemon or lime juice to the ingredients.

Uptown

1 measure lime juice
1 measure orange juice
1 measure pineapple juice
2 measures dark rum
1 dash Cointreau or Triple Sec
1 dash grenadine
1 dash Angostura bitters

Shake ingredients well with crushed ice and pour into a large highball glass or goblet. Decorate with slices of orange, pineapple and lime, with a maraschino cherry and 2 thin straws.

Vanderbilt

1 measure brandy
1 measure cherry brandy
½ measure lemon juice
2 dashes sugar syrup or
½ teaspoon sugar
2 dashes Angostura bitters

This drink should be made in a rocks glass with ice, stirred gently and then decorated with a twist of lemon.
The name of the cocktail commemorates Cornelius Vanderbilt, the American millionaire, who was drowned in the *Lusitania* in 1917.

Whip

1 measure brandy
1 measure dry vermouth
1 measure Pernod
1 measure orange Curaçao

This cocktail should be shaken well with ice. Then strain into a cocktail glass and serve with a twist of orange.

White Rose

1 measure gin
½ measure orange juice
¼ measure lime juice
1 teaspoon sugar
1 egg white

Shake all the ingredients well with ice. Then strain into a cocktail glass. Decorate with a maraschino cherry.

Yellow Fingers

½ measure Galliano
1 measure Southern Comfort
1 measure vodka
1 measure orange juice
Lemonade to top up

Shake ingredients well with ice and pour into a highball glass. Top with lemonade and decorate with a slice of orange and a maraschino cherry.
There is also a cream cocktail of the same name.

Za-Za

1 measure sweet vermouth
1 measure gin
½ measure Cointreau
Orange juice to top up

Pour ingredients over crushed ice in a highball glass and top with orange juice. Decorate with a slice of lemon and a slice of orange.

Exotic Cocktails

Delectable concoctions from the tropics, with the addition of the most exotic of fruits and fruit juices. Tastes to revel in can be tried in cocktails like the Bossa Nova, flavoured with passion fruit, and Ocho Rios, blended with guava.

When the word 'exotic' is put together with 'cocktails' it conjures up a vision of palm-fringed, sun-drenched sands and a palm-thatched beach bar where wonderful concoctions of native fruits and spirits are blended together to produce the most delicious of drinks to help you through the heat of the day – or night.

Rum is naturally the base of the majority of these delightful drinks as most exotic cocktails originate in the Caribbean Islands, South America or Hawaii – sugar-growing areas which produce rum in varying forms. There are of course exceptions: the Margarita from Mexico is made from tequila, and the Hong Kong Fizz, which is said to have originated in a house of ill repute in Hong Kong during the last century, is a potent concoction of several liquors. However, as rum is the primary base, it is useful to know how rum is made, and what types are available.

Rum is a by-product of sugar. When the cane has been picked and crushed, the juice is boiled down and part of this turns to raw or crystallized sugar. Preliminary malting, which turns starch to sugar, is unnecessary as sugar is already present in the cane. The remainder, which is what is known as molasses, is fermented and then finally distilled. As in the production of whisky or brandy, all rums are aged; the youngest type which comes to Britain is usually three years old. Some rums are aged to ten years old and beyond and can attain the velvety smoothness of fine old Cognac.

Although there are many varieties of rum, there are three main types used for cocktails; white (as in Bacardi), light (the colour of whisky) and dark (perhaps the most familiar colour in Europe, although in the Caribbean, light rum is by far the most popular). In the recipes, half white and half dark rum can be substituted for a measure of light rum, if it is not available.

In a tropical climate, all sorts of exotic fruits grow in abundance; it is therefore not suprising that, eventually, delicious fruits such as mangoes, passion fruit and bananas came to be mixed together with coconut milk and blended with rum, thus forming the most well-known of exotic cocktails, the fruit Daquiris and Pinacoladas so popular today. More recently, with the resurgence of interest in cocktails, experimentation with fruit and liquor is on the increase. In America I discovered a delicious new cocktail named 'Julia', consisting of rum, Amaretto, fresh strawberries and cream. When I asked the bartender where he had learned the recipe for this drink, he informed me that it was one of his 'experiments', which should be encouragement to us all.

Acapulco

1 measure light rum
1/4 measure lime juice
1/2 measure Cointreau or Triple Sec
1/2 egg white
1/2 teaspoon sugar
Soda to top up

Shake ingredients well with ice and pour into a highball glass. Top with soda and decorate with 2 fresh mint leaves and 2 thin straws.

Apricot Lady

1 measure light rum
1 measure apricot brandy
1/4 measure orange Curaçao
1/2 egg white
1/2 measure lime juice

Place ingredients with 4–5 ice cubes in a blender and blend for 10 seconds or until smooth. Pour into a rocks glass. Decorate with a slice of orange covering the top of the glass and 2 short thick straws piercing the orange.

Boonoonoos

1 measure light rum
1 measure dark rum
1/4 mango
2 measures orange juice
1 measure lemon juice
3 dashes Angostura bitters
2 dashes grenandine
Soda to top up

Place ingredients in a blender with 4–5 ice cubes and blend until smooth. Pour into a large goblet, about 28cl (1/2 pint). Top with a little soda and decorate with a slice of pineapple speared with a cherry and 2 straws.

Bossa Nova

2 measures dark rum
1/2 measure lime juice
1/2 measure orange juice
56g (2oz or 1/3 cup US) passion fruit or 1 measure of passion fruit juice

Place ingredients in a blender with 4–5 ice cubes and blend for 10 seconds. Pour into a large goblet or highball glass. If necessary top with crushed ice. Decorate with slices of orange and lime speared with a cherry and 2 thick straws.

Corcovado

1 measure blue Curaçao
1 measure tequila
1 measure Drambuie
Lemonade to top up

Shake ingredients well with ice and strain into a highball glass full of crushed ice. Top with lemonade and decorate with a slice of lemon or fresh lime and 2 thin straws.

Left to right **Apricot Lady, Boonoonoos, Corcovado, Acapulco.**

Left to right **Hong Kong Fizz and Julia (both recipes page 56), Havana Beach, Janet Venus (recipe page 56).**

Cuban Peach

1 measure peach brandy
1 measure white rum
$\frac{1}{4}$ measure lime juice
$\frac{1}{4}$ teaspoon sugar

Shake ingredients well with ice and strain into a cocktail glass half full of crushed ice. Float a sprig of fresh mint on top for decoration.

DAQUIRIS

The original Daquiri is basically a white rum sour.

2 measures white rum
1 measure lime juice
$\frac{1}{2}$ teaspoon sugar or
2 dashes sugar syrup

Shake ingredients well with ice and strain into a chilled cocktail glass. Serve with a maraschino cherry.

Fruit Daquiri

Since the advent of the original Daquiri, frozen fruit Daquiris have become increasingly popular. It is advisable to use the same fruit as the fruit liqueur. Any fruit of your choice may be used for flavouring a Daquiri this way, but please remember first to skin the fruit before placing it in a blender, otherwise the cocktail will end up with an extremely bitter taste.

1 measure light rum
1 measure dark rum
1 measure fresh orange juice
56g (2oz or $\frac{1}{3}$ cup US) fruit of your choice
$\frac{1}{2}$ measure fruit liqueur

Place ingredients with 5–6 ice cubes in a blender and blend until smooth. Pour into a large goblet and decorate with 2 thick straws and a slice of pineapple on the side of the glass, speared with a cherry.

Dorothy Lamour

1 measure light rum
1 measure crème de banane
$\frac{1}{2}$ measure mango juice or nectar
$\frac{1}{2}$ measure lime juice

Shake ingredients well with ice and pour into a rocks glass. Decorate with a slice of fresh mango.

East Indies

1 measure brandy
$\frac{1}{2}$ measure orange Curaçao
$\frac{1}{2}$ measure pineapple juice
$\frac{1}{4}$ measure lemon juice
1 dash Angostura bitters
Soda to top up

Shake ingredients well with ice and pour into a highball glass. Top with soda and decorate with chunks of pineapple floating in the drink and a maraschino cherry.

Florida

1 measure white rum
$\frac{1}{4}$ measure green crème de menthe
$\frac{1}{4}$ measure pineapple juice
$\frac{1}{4}$ measure lime juice
Soda to top up

Shake ingredients well with ice. Pour into a highball glass, top with soda and decorate with a sprig of mint.

Fu Manchu

$1\frac{1}{2}$ measures light rum
$\frac{1}{2}$ measure orange Curaçao
$\frac{1}{4}$ measure white crème de menthe
$\frac{1}{4}$ measure lime juice

Shake ingredients well with ice, and strain into a cocktail glass filled with crushed ice. Decorate with a twist of orange.

Golden Gate

1 measure dark rum
$\frac{1}{2}$ measure gin
$\frac{1}{4}$ measure lemon juice
$\frac{1}{4}$ measure dark crème de cacao
1 pinch ginger

Shake ingredients well with ice and pour into a rocks glass. Decorate with a slice of orange.
This is an exceptionally warming drink for cold days.

Havana Beach

2 measures pineapple juice
1 measure white rum
1 teaspoon sugar
$\frac{1}{2}$ fresh lime
Ginger ale to top up

Chop the lime into 4 pieces and place with the other ingredients and ice in a blender and blend until smooth. Pour into a highball glass and top with ginger ale. Decorate with a slice of lime and a cherry.
A delightful drink on a hot summer's day, as the slightly sour lime makes it extremely refreshing.

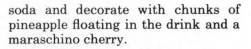

Hong Kong Fizz

½ measure gin
½ measure vodka
½ measure yellow Chartreuse
½ measure green Chartreuse
½ measure Benedictine
½ measure lemon juice
Soda to top up

Shake ingredients well with ice and pour into a large highball glass or goblet. Top with soda and decorate with slices of orange, lemon, lime and a maraschino cherry.
This drink is purported to have been invented by Maude Jones who once ran a famous brothel in Hong Kong in the last century. It is said that she was able to drink 8 or 9 of these before lunch every day – a habit it would be unwise to follow.

Janet Venus

2 measures white rum
1 fresh or canned apricot
½ measure lime juice
½ measure orange Curaçao
Soda to top up

Put all the ingredients in a blender with 4–5 ice cubes and blend until smooth. Pour into a highball glass and top with soda. Decorate with a slice of orange, a maraschino cherry and 2 thin straws.

Julia

1 measure white rum
1 measure Amaretto
1 measure thick cream
56g (2oz or ⅓ cup US) strawberries

Place all the ingredients in a blender with ice and blend until smooth. Pour into a champagne glass or long fluted goblet and decorate with a fresh strawberry. This drink should have the consistency of a milk shake.
For those who have a penchant for strawberries and cream, sipping a Julia slowly through a straw is an undreamed of luxury.

Knickerbocker

½ measure pineapple and raspberry syrup or juice, mixed
½ measure lemon and orange juice, mixed
2 measures light rum

Shake ingredients well with ice and pour into a rocks glass. Decorate with a slice of pineapple and slices of other available fruit.

Larchmont

2 measures white rum
1 measure Grand Marnier
½ measure lime juice

Shake ingredients well with ice and pour into a rocks glass with crushed ice. Decorate with a twist of orange peel.

Leeward

1 measure light rum
½ measure Calvados
½ measure sweet vermouth

Shake ingredients well with ice and strain into a rocks glass over crushed ice. Decorate with a twist of lemon.

Mai Tai

There are several different versions of the Mai Tai, but this seems to be the most popular with bartenders and patrons alike.

½ measure dark rum
1 measure light rum
½ measure tequila
½ measure Triple Sec
1 measure apricot brandy
1 measure orange juice
1 dash orgeat
1 dash Angostura bitters
2 dashes grenadine

Put all the ingredients in a blender with a little ice and blend until smooth. Pour into a large goblet or tankard. Decorate with slices of orange, lime, lemon and pineapple and a maraschino cherry.
This drink will taste deliciously innocuous, but beware! It has a habit of creeping up on you.

Mandeville

2 measures dark rum
½ measure lemon juice
1 teaspoon Pernod
¼ teaspoon grenadine
Coca-Cola to top up

Shake ingredients well with ice and pour into a rocks glass. Top with Coca-Cola and decorate with an orange slice.

Margarita

1½ measures tequila
1 measure Triple Sec
½ measure lemon juice

Shake ingredients well with ice and strain into a salt-rimmed cocktail glass.
The ideal way to rim the glass with salt is, first, to rub the inside and outer edge with a wedge of lemon and then dip the glass evenly and gently in a saucer of fine salt. The art of salting is to make sure that the rim of salt is neither too thick nor too thin.
Some aficianados of the Margarita prefer to use a mixture of lime and lemon juice in the preparation, but this is left to personal taste. Whichever way you like it, this drink has an exceptional bite to it.

Muskmelon

1 measure light rum
¼ cup diced ripe melon
¼ measure lime juice
¼ measure orange juice

Put all the ingredients in a blender with 4–5 ice cubes and blend until smooth. Pour into a hollowed-out half of a small melon shell or a large goblet. Top with ice cubes, if desired. Decorate with 2 thick straws.
When hollowing out the melon, ensure that there is enough meat left in the shell to enable it to remain firm once the cocktail has been poured into it.

Ocho Rios

1 measure dark rum
1 measure guava juice or ½ cup diced guava
¼ measure lime juice

Put all the ingredients in a blender with 4–5 ice cubes and blend until smooth. Pour into a champagne glass.

Left to right **Larchmont, Margarita, Mai Tai.**

Petite Fleur

1 measure white rum
1 measure Cointreau or Triple Sec
1 measure grapefruit juice

Shake ingredients well together with ice and strain into a chilled cocktail glass. Decorate with a twist of orange peel.

Pinacolada

Outside the Caribbean it seems very difficult to find a bar that can produce this cocktail properly, because the drink requires fresh coconut rather than canned. Although the following recipe may not be entirely traditional, it seems to be close to the taste of a Caribbean Pinacolada.

2 measures white rum
2 measures pineapple juice or ½ cup diced pineapple
2 teaspoons coconut milk or meat
2 dashes Angostura bitters
1 pinch salt

Place all the ingredients in a blender with 4–5 ice cubes and blend until smooth. Pour into a semi-hollowed pineapple husk or large goblet. Decorate with a slice of pineapple and a maraschino cherry.

Planter's Punch

2 measures light rum
½ measure grenadine
1 measure lime juice
1 measure orange juice
2 dashes Angostura bitters

Fill a highball glass with ice, pour in all the ingredients and stir well. Top with soda. Decorate with half slices of orange, lime, lemon and maraschino cherries floating in the drink.

Quarter Deck

This is an old navy drink, as you may have guessed from the name.

2 measures dark rum
1 measure dry sherry
1 dash lime juice

Fill a rocks glass with ice and pour the ingredients over the ice in the order they appear above. Decorate with a wedge of fresh lime.

Rumba

1 measure dark rum
½ measure light rum
½ measure gin
1 measure lime and lemon juice, mixed
2 dashes grenadine

Shake ingredients with ice, then pour into a highball glass and top with soda. Decorate with a slice of lemon and lime, speared with a cherry.
This may not taste strong, but it is liquid dynamite!

Left to right **Pinacolada, Muskmelon (recipe page 56), Petite Fleur.**

San Juan

1 measure light rum
¾ measure grapefruit juice
1 teaspoon coconut milk
2 teaspoons lime juice

Place ingredients in a blender with ice and blend until smooth. Pour into a champagne glass and float brandy on the top. Decorate with a twist of lime.

Santiago

1 measure orange Curaçao
1 measure lime juice
2 measures white rum
2 dashes Angostura bitters

Mix ingredients in a rocks glass with ice and decorate with a wedge of fresh orange.

Scorpion

2 measures light rum
1 measure orange juice
1 measure lemon juice
½ measure brandy
¼ measure orgeat syrup

Place ingredients in a blender with ice and blend until smooth. Pour into a rocks glass and fill with ice cubes. Decorate with a slice of orange and a sprig of mint.

Shark's Tooth

1 measure dark rum
1 dash lemon juice
1 dash cerise or cherry brandy
1 dash sweet vermouth
1 dash sloe gin
1 dash Angostura bitters

Shake ingredients well with ice and strain into a cocktail glass. Decorate with a twist of orange and a cherry.

Sinful Sadie

1 measure light rum
¼ measure crème de banane
¼ measure orange juice
½ egg white
½ teaspoon grenadine

Put all the ingredients in a blender with ice and blend until smooth. Pour into a champagne glass and decorate with a slice of lime, speared with a cherry.

Sunset in Paradise

1 measure dark rum
1 teaspoon brown sugar
½ measure lime juice
¼ measure Triple Sec or Cointreau
¼ measure sweet vermouth

Put all the ingredients in a blender with ice and blend until smooth. Pour into a champagne glass and decorate with a twist of orange and a maraschino cherry.

Tequador

1 measure tequila
$1\frac{1}{2}$ measures pineapple juice
$\frac{1}{4}$ measure lime juice
Grenadine

Shake the tequila and fruit juices well with ice and pour over crushed ice into a rocks glass. Fill with more crushed ice and then add three drops of grenadine in the centre of the drink.

Tequila Sunrise

1 measure tequila
Orange juice
1 teaspoon grenadine

Fill a highball glass with ice cubes and add tequila. Pour in orange juice to within 12mm ($\frac{1}{2}$in) of the top of the glass. Add the grenadine which will sink to the bottom of the glass and then partly permeate the orange juice.

Tobago

1 measure light rum
1 measure gin
1 measure lime juice
$\frac{1}{2}$ measure guava syrup

Put all the ingredients in a blender with 4 ice cubes and blend until smooth. Pour into an old fashioned glass and decorate with a twist of lime peel.

Trade Winds

1 measure light rum
$\frac{1}{4}$ measure lime juice
$\frac{1}{4}$ measure sloe gin
1 teaspoon sugar

Shake ingredients well with ice and pour into a cocktail glass filled with crushed ice. Decorate with a black cherry.

Viva Maria

1 measure tequila
$\frac{1}{2}$ measure lime juice
$\frac{1}{2}$ egg white
$\frac{1}{4}$ measure maraschino liqueur
$\frac{1}{2}$ teaspoon grenadine

Shake ingredients well with ice and strain into a champagne glass filled with crushed ice. Decorate with a slice of lemon and a maraschino cherry.

Zombie

1 measure dark rum
1 measure light rum
1 measure apricot brandy
$\frac{1}{2}$ measure lemon juice
$\frac{1}{2}$ measure pineapple juice
$\frac{1}{2}$ measure orange juice

Place ingredients in a blender with ice and blend until smooth. Pour into a large goblet or tankard and top with crushed ice. Decorate with slices of pineapple, orange, lemon, lime and a maraschino cherry.

Cream Cocktails

A favourite liqueur mixed with thick rich cream – what could be more luxurious for those not on a diet! Expensive ingredients, but worth it to make a deliciously smooth drink at the end of an evening.

Cream cocktails should be enjoyed for their smoothness and richness, particularly pleasing as an end of the evening drink. Although they are usually served after a meal, they can be drunk at any time, and indeed a Brandy Alexander or Grasshopper may be extremely refreshing served at midday.

It is unknown when cream cocktails made their advent, but it seems that they may have evolved naturally from the egg nogs and punches of the Elizabethan era. Cream mixes with most liqueurs and it is great fun to experiment and invent a cream cocktail of your own. The main drawbacks of cream cocktails are the cost of producing them, as the ingredients are expensive; their richness, which means drawing upon reserves of self-restraint, otherwise nausea ensues; and, of course, cream cocktails have the highest calorific value of all cocktails, so they are to be avoided by anyone on a diet.

The cream used in cocktails should be thick or 'double' cream. Some bartenders prefer to use the thinner single cream, but this usually leaves the finished cocktail looking like a rather runny milkshake. The cream should always be fresh and if it is more than a day or two old, ensure that it has not gone sour. It is also important to note that when mixing cream with fruit juices, it is best to mix the cocktail immediately the drink is to be served, rather than to let the cocktail stand, otherwise the action of the acid in the fruit on the cream will make it curdle.

When storing cream, either leave the cream in the container in which it was purchased, or transfer it to a glass jug or container. Do not use metal containers to store cream as there is always a danger of the metal tainting the cream.

Another important point to remember is always to wash out the shaker immediately after you have produced a cream cocktail. Cream deteriorates rapidly when not refrigerated and will easily contaminate the shaker and spoil your next cocktail. It is very important to keep bar equipment scrupulously clean and this will be ensured if you make a habit of cleaning the equipment you have used immediately after making each cocktail.

When serving a cream cocktail it is sometimes a nice touch to frost the rim of the glass with sugar. The way to do this is explained in 'Tricks of the Trade'.

In the structure of a cream cocktail, cream is the modifying agent: its basic purpose is to remove the harshness of the alcohol, leaving a palatable drink with a thick, smooth texture which slides gently down the throat.

ALEXANDERS

Brandy Alexander

1 measure brandy
*1 measure crème de cacao or **Tia Maria***
1 measure cream

Shake ingredients well with ice and strain into a cocktail or champagne glass. A finishing touch to a Brandy Alexander may be the sprinkling of finely grated nutmeg on top of the completed cocktail.

Gin Alexander

1 measure gin
*1 measure crème de cacao or **Tia Maria***
1 measure cream

Shake ingredients well with ice and strain into a cocktail or champagne glass.

Banana Bliss

1 measure white rum
1 measure crème de banane
½ measure orange juice
1 dash Angostura bitters
Grenadine
1 measure cream

Shake ingredients well with ice and pour into a rocks glass. Add a few drops of grenadine to the top of the drink and garnish with a few slices of banana.

Blue Angel

½ measure blue Curaçao
½ measure Parfait d'amour
1 measure brandy
1 dash lemon juice
1 measure cream

Shake ingredients well with ice and strain into a cocktail glass. This makes a cool and incredibly smooth blend.

Blue Hawaii

1 measure white rum
½ measure blue Curaçao
½ measure Cointreau or Triple Sec
1 measure cream

Shake ingredients well with ice and strain into a cocktail glass or pour into a rocks glass. A delightful post-dinner cocktail for a warm summer's night.

Cara Sposa

1 measure Tia Maria
1 measure orange Curaçao
1 measure cream

Place ingredients with 3–4 ice cubes into a blender and blend for 10 seconds. Pour into a champagne saucer with the edge frosted with sugar and a slice of orange on the side.

Left to right **Caribbean Creole (recipe page 64), Brandy Alexander, Blue Hawaii, Cumparasita (recipe page 64).**

Caribbean Creole

1 measure light rum
½ measure lime juice
2 dashes grenadine
½ measure cream

Shake ingredients well with ice and strain into a cocktail glass filled with crushed ice. Garnish with a black cherry and leaf of fresh mint.

Cumparasita

1 measure brandy
1 measure apricot brandy
1 measure orange juice
¼ measure kirsch
¼ measure dry vermouth
1 measure cream

Fill a highball glass with ice and pour ingredients over ice. Stir until the liquors have mixed well, add a dash of grenadine and let it float through the drink. Garnish with 2 thin straws, and a slice of orange on the side of the glass speared with a cherry.

Deb's Delight

1 measure vodka
1 measure apricot brandy
½ measure anisette
Cream

Mix all ingredients except cream with ice in a mixing glass and pour into a rocks glass. Pour cream over the ice until just below the rim of the glass.

Dizzy Dame

1 measure brandy
1 measure Kahlua
1 dash cherry brandy
1 measure cream

Shake ingredients well with ice and pour into a rocks glass. Garnish with a cherry and two small straws.

Golden Cadillac

1 measure Cointreau or Triple Sec
1 measure white crème de cacao
½ measure orange juice
2 dashes Galliano
1 measure cream

Shake ingredients well with ice and strain into a cocktail glass.

Golden Dream

This is another version of the Golden Cadillac with the omission of the Galliano. Make in the same way and serve in a cocktail glass.

Grasshopper

1 measure green crème de menthe
1 measure white crème de cacao
1 measure cream

Shake ingredients well with ice and strain into a cocktail glass. Decorate with finely grated chocolate on top of the drink. With its minty taste, this is one of the most refreshing cream cocktails.

Imagination

½ measure coconut milk
½ measure orange Curaçao
¼ measure tequila
½ measure cream

Shake ingredients well with ice and strain into a cocktail glass filled with crushed ice.

Justine

1 measure vodka
½ measure crème de noyaux
2 dashes orgeat
½ measure kirsch
1 measure cream

Shake ingredients well with ice and strain into a cocktail glass.

Kahlua Kiss

Kahlua
1 dash crème de noyaux
Cream

Fill a cocktail glass with crushed ice and half fill with Kahlua. Add a dash of crème de noyaux and then float cream on top.
An excellent drink for the end of an enjoyable evening.

Leroy Washington

1 measure brandy
½ measure Tia Maria
½ measure Drambuie
1 measure cream

Shake ingredients well with ice and strain into a cocktail glass.

Mandarin

½ measure apricot brandy
½ measure Benedictine
¼ measure Galliano
¼ measure orange Curaçao
1 measure orange juice
1 measure cream

Shake ingredients well with ice and pour into a highball glass. Add ice until glass is three-quarters full. Garnish with a slice of orange speared with a cherry.

Manetti

½ measure gin
½ measure Calvados
½ measure Cointreau or Triple Sec
1 dash grenadine
1 dash lemon juice
1 measure cream

Shake ingredients well with ice and strain into a cocktail glass.

Matinée

1 measure gin
½ measure Sambuca
½ egg white
1 dash lime juice
½ measure cream

Shake ingredients well with ice and strain into a cocktail glass. Garnish with finely grated nutmeg on top of the cocktail.

New Orleans Gin Fizz

2 measures gin
1 measure sugar syrup
1 measure lemon juice
1 measure lime juice
1 egg white
½ measure cream
Soda to top up

Shake ingredients well with crushed ice, strain into a highball glass and top with soda. Decorate with a slice of lemon or fresh lime and 2 straws. This drink should still be quite thick after the soda has been added.

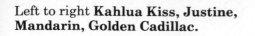
Left to right **Kahlua Kiss, Justine, Mandarin, Golden Cadillac.**

Orsini

½ *measure gin*
2 *measures orange juice*
1 *measure orange Curaçao*
¼ *measure lemon juice*
1 *dash Angostura bitters*
2 *measures cream*

Place ingredients into a blender with 5–6 cubes of ice and blend until smooth. Pour into a highball glass. Garnish with two thin straws and a slice of orange on the side of the glass.

Pink Lady

1 *measure gin*
1 *dash lime juice*
2 *dashes grenadine*
½ *egg white*
½ *measure cream*

Shake ingredients well with ice and strain into a cocktail glass. Frost the rim beforehand by dipping it into grenadine and then into sugar.

Pink Squirrel

1 measure crême de noyaux
1 measure white crême de cacao
1 measure cream

Shake ingredients well with ice and strain into a cocktail glass.

Pompeii

1 measure brandy
½ measure white crême de cacao
½ measure Amaretto
1 measure cream

Shake ingredients well with cream and strain into a champagne saucer. Decorate with lightly flaked almonds floated on top of the cocktail.

Renaissance

1 measure gin
½ measure dry sherry
½ measure cream

Shake ingredients well with ice and strain into a cocktail glass filled with crushed ice. Garnish with a little finely grated nutmeg on top of the cocktail.

Sarabande

2 measures orange juice
1 measure gin
1 measure crême de cacao
½ egg white
1 measure cream

Place ingredients in a blender with ice and blend until mixture is smooth, but light and frothy. Pour into a large goblet or highball glass. Decorate with a slice of orange on the side of the glass and some finely grated chocolate on top of the cocktail. Also garnish with two straws.
A long, cool, creamy drink for summer afternoons and early evenings.

Scotch Solace

1 measure Scotch whisky
1 teaspoon honey
½ measure Cointreau or Triple Sec
14cl (¼ pint or ⅔ cup US) milk
1 measure cream

Fill a highball glass with ice and pour in whisky, honey and Triple Sec or Cointreau. When thoroughly mixed and the honey has dissolved, add milk, cream and a little grated orange peel.

Silver Jubilee

1 measure gin
1 measure crême de banane
1 measure cream

Shake ingredients well with ice and pour into a rocks glass. Garnish with three slices of banana on top of the cocktail and a slice of orange on the side of the glass.

Southern Peach

1 measure Southern Comfort
1 measure peach brandy
1 dash Angostura bitters
1 measure cream

Shake ingredients well with ice and strain into a cocktail glass. Alternatively the drink can be poured into a rocks glass and a slice of fresh peach may be used as a garnish.

Once you have tasted this, peaches and cream will never be the same again!

Strawberry Cream Cooler

1 measure gin
¼ cup canned or frozen strawberries
½ measure lemon juice
1 teaspoon sugar
1½ measures cream

Place ingredients in a blender without ice and blend at a high speed for 10 seconds. Pour into a highball glass or large goblet. Add a splash of soda and then top with ice cubes. Decorate with a large strawberry on the side of the glass and two thick straws.

Strawberry Dream

1 measure fraise
¼ measure kirsch
½ measure light rum
1 measure cream

Shake ingredients well with ice and pour into a rocks glass. Decorate with a large strawberry floating in the cocktail and two short straws.

Sweet Dreams

1 measure apricot brandy
1 measure pineapple juice
½ measure gin
1 measure light rum
1 measure cream

Place ingredients in a blender with 5–6 cubes of ice. Blend for 10 seconds and pour into a highball glass. Garnish with two straws and a large twist of orange peel.

Theodore

1 measure light rum
½ measure brandy
1 measure Advocaat
1 measure orange juice
2 measures milk
½ teaspoon sugar
1 measure cream

Place ingredients in a blender with 4–5 ice cubes and blend until smooth. Pour into a large goblet or highball glass. Garnish with a little grated cinnamon sprinkled on the top of the cocktail.

Tijuana Coffee

1 measure Kahlua
2 demi-tasse cups hot black coffee
14cl (¼ pint or ⅔ cup US) whipped cream

Pour the Kahlua and coffee into a 23cl (8oz) goblet. Stir in the whipped cream. Sprinkle with cinnamon.

Velvet Hammer

½ measure brandy
½ measure Tia Maria
1 measure Cointreau or Triple Sec
1 measure cream

Shake ingredients well with ice and strain into a cocktail glass.

The name of the cocktail tells all – a smooth cocktail that has quite a punch!

White Russian

1 measure Kahlua
1 measure vodka
Cream

Fill a rocks glass with ice, pour in the vodka and Kahlua and then top with cream.

A Black Russian is basically a White Russian without cream; for the recipe see 'Traditional Cocktails'.

Xaviera

½ measure crème de noyaux
½ measure Kahlua
½ measure orange Curaçao
1 measure cream

Shake ingredients well with ice and strain into a cocktail glass. Top with crushed ice.

Yellow Fingers

1 measure gin
1 measure blackberry brandy
½ measure crème de banane
½ measure cream

Shake ingredients well with ice and strain into a champagne saucer.

There is a recipe for a totally different concoction with the same name in 'Traditional Cocktails'.

Zia Maria

1 measure Tia Maria
½ measure orange Curaçao
1 dash Galliano
1 measure cream

Shake ingredients well with ice and strain into a cocktail glass filled with crushed ice.

Wine Concoctions

A chilled champagne cocktail to tickle the palate, a refreshing Kir on a warm day, Port in a Storm for a cold one – the range of wine cocktails is as wide as the number of wines, fortified or not, on the market.

There are a great variety of wines to choose from for wine cocktails. Apart from the wide range of table wines there are the fortified wines – ports, sherries, vermouths and of course, champagne.

Many of the recipes given here are champagne cocktails. Like all cocktails they can be enjoyed any time, but are marvellous served in the morning or just before a meal. A good champagne breakfast is a Buck's Fizz with Eggs Benedict.

Always chill champagne before making the cocktails. When opening the bottle, ease out the cork by holding it firmly with one hand and turning round the base of the bottle with the other. Remember when making your cocktails, never to put champagne in a blender – it would cause an explosion. If your pocket does not stretch to champagne, top up your cocktails with a chilled dry sparkling wine – it tastes just as good. Any champagne or wine left over can be kept in the refrigerator for several days, if the bottle has been corked with a spring-loaded metal top.

Wine cocktails should always be served in clear glasses to show off their colour and sparkle. For champagne cocktails use a champagne saucer, or, better still, a tall narrow champagne glass which holds in the bubbles longer.

Vermouths are excellent modifying agents in wine cocktails – although they have earned their fame in the making of Martinis. There is a good range of different types on the market.

Sherry will make a cocktail base, but at only half the strength of a spirit it will not have the same punch. For cocktails it is best to use a dry sherry, unless you are making a Flip, in which case use a cream sherry. Port also makes a cocktail base, but tends to be sweet despite its range. When experimenting, be careful about the amounts of sherry and port you use, as their flavours are strong and tend to overpower the other ingredients.

Table wines are very versatile, mixing with most liqueurs. White wine can be made into a cocktail by the simple addition of a syrup. Once again use a dry wine as the other ingredients in the cocktail tend to be sweet.

The range of wine and champagne makes experimenting fun. Here follow a few recipes to help you on your way.

Alfonso

1 measure sweet vermouth
½ teaspoon sugar
2 dashes Angostura bitters
Champagne

Half fill a highball glass with ice and add the sugar, Angostura bitters and vermouth. Stir well and top with champagne. Garnish with a twist of lemon.

Americana

1 measure Bourbon whiskey
½ teaspoon sugar
1 dash Angostura bitters
Champagne

Stir Bourbon, sugar and bitters in a champagne glass until sugar has dissolved. Then top with champagne and garnish with a slice of peach.

Apple Pie

1 measure sweet vermouth
3 measures apple juice
½ measure lime juice
Soda to top up

Place ingredients in a blender with 5–6 cubes of ice and blend for 10 seconds. Pour into a large goblet and top with soda. Garnish with a ring of apple and slice of lemon on the side of the glass.

Bellini

3 measures peach juice or nectar
Champagne

Place the peach juice or peach nectar in a blender with 5–6 ice cubes and blend until ice is roughly crushed. Pour into a large goblet and then top with champagne. Garnish with slices of peach.

Beretta

1 measure dry vermouth
½ measure gin
½ measure orange Curaçao
3 measures medium white wine
2 dashes Angostura bitters

Mix ingredients in a mixing glass with ice and pour into a large goblet or highball glass.

Buck's Fizz

Orange juice
Champagne

Fill a highball glass with crushed ice and then quarter fill with orange juice. Top with champagne and float a half slice of orange on the top of the drink.

Left to right **Bellini, Beretta, Buck's Fizz, Apple Pie.**

Burlington

1 measure sweet vermouth
1 measure Calvados
2 measures red wine
Soda to top up

Mix ingredients in a mixing glass with ice and pour into a highball glass. Top with soda. Decorate with a slice of orange and 2 thin straws.

California Dreaming

3 measures pineapple juice
2 dashes kirsch
1 dash lemon juice
Champagne

Place the kirsch and juices in a blender with 4–5 cubes of ice and blend for 10 seconds. Pour into a large goblet and top with champagne. Garnish with a slice of fresh pineapple on the side of the glass and 2 straws.

Caribbean Champagne

¼ measure light rum
¼ measure crême de banane
1 dash Angostura bitters
Champagne

Pour rum, banana liqueur and bitters into a champagne glass. Top with champagne and stir gently. Garnish with a slice of banana speared with a cherry.

Champagne Normande

1 teaspoon Calvados
½ teaspoon sugar
1 dash Angostura bitters
Champagne

Put Calvados, sugar and bitters in a champagne glass and stir until sugar has dissolved. Top with champagne, and decorate with a slice of orange.

Classic Champagne Cocktail

1 sugar cube
1 dash Angostura bitters
Champagne

Place the sugar cube in a champagne glass and pour the bitters on it.

Top with champagne and decorate with a twist of lemon peel. This may be enhanced by the addition of a measure of orange Curaçao, with brandy floated on the top.

Cool Cucumber

1 measure Benedictine
½ measure lemon juice
Cucumber
Champagne

Place 3 ice cubes in a highball glass and pour in the Benedictine and lemon juice. Cut a strip of cucumber with the peel the length of the glass and place inside the glass. Top with champagne and stir with the slice of cucumber. Leave the drink to settle for 2–3 minutes to allow the flavour of the cucumber to permeate.

Coronation

1 measure dry sherry
1 measure dry vermouth
1 dash maraschino
2 dashes Angostura bitters
3 measures medium white wine
Soda to top up

Mix well with ice in a mixing glass and pour into a large goblet or highball glass. Top with soda.

Damn the Weather

1 measure port
½ measure pineapple juice
½ measure orange juice
1 dash lemon juice
Soda to top up

Shake ingredients well with ice and pour into a large goblet. Top with soda and garnish with slices of orange, lemon and pineapple and 2 straws.

East and West

½ measure port
½ measure brandy
½ measure orange Curaçao
¼ measure lemon juice

Shake ingredients well with ice and strain into a rocks glass filled with crushed ice. Garnish with a slice of lemon and slice of orange and 2 small straws.

Left to right **Classic Champagne Cocktail, Coronation, California Dreaming, Cool Cucumber.**

Granada

1 measure dry sherry
1 measure brandy
½ measure orange Curaçao
Tonic water to top up

Mix ingredients well with ice in a mixing glass and pour into a highball glass. Top up with tonic water and garnish with a slice of orange and 2 thin straws.

Greenbriar

2 measures dry sherry
1 measure dry vermouth
1 dash Angostura bitters

Mix ingredients well with ice in a mixing glass and pour into a rocks glass. If necessary top with ice cubes and garnish with a sprig of fresh mint.

Happy Hollander

½ measure white rum
1 measure mango nectar
½ measure maraschino
1 dash lemon juice
¼ teaspoon sugar
Champagne

Shake all ingredients, except champagne, well with ice and strain into a tall glass half filled with crushed ice. Top with champagne and garnish with a slice of lemon and 2 straws.

Happy Youth

1 measure cherry brandy
3 measures orange juice
Champagne

Pour the cherry brandy and orange juice over ice into a large goblet and top with champagne. Garnish with a slice of orange speared with a cherry.

Henry's Special

2 measures grapefruit juice
½ measure lemon juice
2 teaspoons honey
1 measure brandy
Champagne

Place all ingredients, except champagne, in a blender and blend with 3–4 ice cubes for 20 seconds. Pour into a large goblet or highball glass and top up with champagne and ice cubes.

Honeydew

¼ cup diced honeydew melon
1 measure gin
1 dash Pernod
½ measure lemon juice
Champagne

Place all ingredients, except champagne, in a blender with 3–4 ice cubes and blend for 10 seconds. Then pour into a large goblet. Top with champagne and decorate with a wedge of melon.

Imelda

1 measure cream sherry
½ measure kirsch
½ measure lemon juice
½ measure orange juice
Champagne

Place sherry, kirsch and lemon and orange juice in a blender with 3–4 cubes of ice and blend for 10 seconds. Pour into a large goblet or tumbler and top with champagne. Decorate with slices of orange, pineapple and lemon speared with a cherry.

Inigo Jones

1 measure Marsala
1 measure brandy
1 measure rosé wine
1 dash lemon juice
1 dash orange juice

Place ingredients in a mixing glass and mix well. Strain into a rocks glass half filled with crushed ice. Garnish with half a slice of orange floating on the top of the cocktail.

Kir

White wine
½ measure cassis

Three-quarters fill a large wine glass with chilled white wine, then add the cassis and stir gently. The usual ratio of wine to cassis is 7:1.

Left to right **Happy Hollander, Imelda, Never on Sunday, Kir, Montmartre.**

Light 'n' Dry

1 measure dry sherry
½ measure brandy
½ measure light rum
1 dash Angostura bitters

Stir ingredients well with ice in a mixing glass. Strain into a cocktail glass. Top with finely crushed ice.

Maxim's à Londres

1 measure brandy
¼ measure Cointreau or Triple Sec
¼ measure orange juice
Champagne

Mix the brandy, Cointreau and orange juice well with ice in a mixing glass and strain into a champagne glass. Top with champagne and garnish with a twist of orange.

Montmartre

1 measure brandy
½ measure yellow Chartreuse
1 dash lemon juice
1 dash Angostura bitters
Champagne

Shake the brandy, Chartreuse, lemon juice and Angostura bitters well with ice, pour into a rocks glass and top with champagne. Garnish with a cherry and 2 short straws.

Never on Sunday

1 measure Greek brandy (Metaxa)
½ measure ouzo
1 dash Angostura bitters
1 dash lemon juice
Ginger beer and champagne mixed to top up

Mix ingredients well with ice in a mixing glass and pour into a highball glass. Top with ginger beer and champagne mixed.

New Orleans Dandy

1 measure light rum
1 dash orange juice
1 dash lime juice
½ measure peach brandy
Champagne

Shake the rum, peach brandy and juices well with ice and pour into a large goblet or highball glass. Top with champagne. Decorate with a slice of orange and a cherry.

Left to right **Port in a Storm, Operator, Pink Chevrolet, White Wine Cooler.**

Operator

5 measures white wine
1 dash lime juice
Ginger ale to top up

Pour white wine and lime juice over ice into a highball glass and top with ginger ale. Decorate with a slice of fresh lime or lemon and 2 thin straws.

Pineapple Cooler

85g (3oz or ½ cup US) diced pineapple
3 measures white wine
1 dash lemon juice
Soda to top up

Place ingredients in a blender with 3–4 ice cubes or until smooth. Pour into a large goblet and top with soda.

Pink Chevrolet

56g (2oz or ⅓ cup US) fresh strawberries
1 measure fraise
1 dash lemon juice
Champagne

Place the strawberries, fraise and lemon juice with 3–4 ice cubes in a blender and blend for 10 seconds, or until smooth. Pour into a highball glass and top with champagne. Decorate with a fresh strawberry.

Port in a Storm

1½ measures port
½ measure brandy
2 measures light red wine

Mix ingredients well with ice and pour into a large goblet. Add more ice to top up and garnish with twists of orange and lemon and a sprig of fresh mint.

Restoration

2 measures red wine
½ measure brandy
½ measure framboise
1 dash lemon juice
Soda to top up

Pour ingredients into a highball glass half filled with ice. Stir well until all ingredients are mixed together. Fill glass with soda and float 2–3 raspberries on top.

Roman Holiday

½ measure gin
½ measure sweet vermouth
1 dash lemon juice
Dry white wine

Shake the gin, vermouth and lemon juice well with ice and pour into a rocks glass. Top with dry Italian white wine and garnish with a twist of lemon.

San Juan Sparkler

½ measure white rum
½ measure cherry brandy
¼ measure Benedictine
1 dash lime juice
1 dash Angostura bitters
Champagne

Shake all the ingredients, except the champagne, well with ice and pour into a highball glass. Top with champagne.

White Wine Cooler

3 measures dry white wine
½ measure brandy
1 dash Angostura bitters
1 dash kummel
½ teaspoon sugar
Soda to top up

Shake ingredients well together with ice and pour into a large goblet or highball glass. Top with soda and garnish with a twist of cucumber peel.

Non-Alcoholic Cocktails

Teetotallers need not suffer – there are many 'mocktails' you can make using all sorts of fruit juices and tonic waters. Or experiment by blending in fruit. These drinks are deliciously refreshing, if not as exhilarating, as an alcoholic cocktail!

Days of Prohibition! When bathtub gin and whisky came 'straight off the boat' – which meant straight off the ferry into New York. Although illegal selling of alcohol was rife in the United States in those days, there were many people who seemed quite content to forgo alcoholic beverages and make their non-alcoholic mixes or 'mocktails'. Many of the recipes that are in use today stem from those days of Prohibition, although, of course, fruit punch or fruit cups made without alcohol have been in use for many years.

There are still many people who for reasons of health or diet do not drink alcohol. However, their presence at a cocktail party need not make either you or them miserable. With the ready availability nowadays of exotic fruit and non-alcoholic syrups such as grenadine, cassis, cerise, framboise, fraise, etc, delightful concoctions can be made. They can be either shaken or blended to a near water ice consistency, and then topped up with soda, or low-calorie tonic waters and lemonade, and decorated with fruit. These cocktails can be equally as delicious, if not as efficacious, as an alcoholic cocktail.

Anita

3 measures orange juice
1 measure lemon juice
3 dashes Angostura bitters
Soda to top up

Shake ingredients well with ice, pour into a highball glass and top with soda. Decorate with slices of orange and lemon with 2 straws.

Appleade

½ teaspoon sugar
2 large apples
57cl (1 pint or 2½ cups US) boiling water

Roughly dice the apples and pour the boiling water over them. Add the sugar and strain into a jug. Allow to cool. When cooled, pour into a highball glass half full of ice and serve. Decorate with a slice of apple and 2 straws.

Capucine

½ measure peppermint cordial
2 measures cream

Shake peppermint and cream well with ice and strain into a champagne saucer. Top with crushed ice and sprinkle with finely grated chocolate.

Cardinal Punch

2 measures cranberry juice
1 measure orange juice
½ measure lemon juice
Ginger ale to top up

Pour all the juices into a large goblet half filled with ice cubes and then top with ginger ale. Decorate with slices of orange and lemon and 2 thin straws.

Cartland Cure

1 egg
1 banana
2 dessertspoons yoghurt
1 teaspoon honey
1 teaspoon wheatgerm
1 teaspoon lecithin
2 measures milk

Place all ingredients in a blender and blend until smooth. Pour into a large goblet or highball glass and sprinkle the top with crushed hazelnuts.

Cinderella

1 measure lemon juice
1 measure pineapple juice
1 measure orange juice
1 dash grenadine
Soda to top up

Shake all the juices well with ice and pour into a highball glass. Top with soda and then add a dash of grenadine. Decorate with a slice of pineapple and 2 thin straws.

Left to right **Grecian (recipe page 81), Anita, Cardinal Punch.**

78

Left to right **Princess Margaret, Limey, Jersey Lily, Parson's Particular.**

Dot's Hot Spot

½ wine glass grape juice
½ wine glass apple juice
½ stick cinnamon
1 teaspoon honey

Heat ingredients in a saucepan for 4–5 minutes. Allow to cool slightly and pour into a rocks glass. Decorate with a slice of lemon floating on the top of the drink.

Godchild

1 measure cassis
1 dash lemon juice
Lemonade or soda

Fill a highball glass with ice, then pour in lemonade until the glass is three-quarters full. Add lemon juice and cassis to float on the top. Decorate with a slice of lemon and 2 straws.

Grecian

2 measures peach juice
1 measure orange juice
½ measure lemon juice

Blend all ingredients well with ice until smooth and pour into a large goblet. Top with soda and decorate with slices of orange, lemon and lime.

Himbeersaft

2 measures raspberry syrup
Soda to top up

Fill a highball glass with crushed ice and then add the raspberry syrup. Top with soda, and stir until the syrup is mixed well with the soda. Decorate with a sprig of mint and 2 straws.

Horsefeathers

¼ measure lemon juice
1 dash Tabasco sauce
1 dash Worcestershire sauce
Pinch of salt
Consommé

Half fill a large goblet with ice and then add all the ingredients. Pour from the glass into the mixing glass and back again; repeat this twice. Decorate with a stick of celery.

Jersey Lily

1 wine glass carbonated apple juice
2 dashes Angostura bitters
¼ teaspoon sugar

Stir ingredients with ice in a mixing glass and strain back into the wine glass. Decorate with a maraschino cherry.

Limey

1 measure lime juice
½ measure lemon juice
½ egg white

Shake ingredients well with ice and strain into a cocktail glass. Decorate with a maraschino cherry.

Nursery Fizz

Orange juice
Ginger ale

Fill a large goblet with ice and pour in equal parts of orange juice and ginger ale. Decorate with a slice of orange speared with a cherry and 2 straws.

Parson's Particular

2 measures fresh orange juice
1 measure fresh lemon juice
1 egg yolk
4 dashes grenadine

Shake ingredients well with ice and then strain into a cocktail glass. Serve decorated with a maraschino cherry.

Pom Pom

1 egg white
1 measure lemon juice
1 dash grenadine
Lemonade to top up

Shake well with ice, then strain over crushed ice into a champagne glass. Top with lemonade.

Prairie Oyster II

2 teaspoons tomato juice
1 egg yolk
2 dashes wine vinegar
Pepper
1 teaspoon Worcestershire sauce
1 dash Tabasco sauce

Place all ingredients in a wine glass and stir carefully so as not to break the egg yolk; then serve.
For Prairie Oyster I, the alcoholic version, see 'Tricks of the Trade'.

Princess Margaret

5 large strawberries
1 slice pineapple
Juice of ½ lemon
Juice of ½ orange
2 dashes fraise

Place ingredients in a blender with 4–5 ice cubes and blend until smooth. Pour into a highball glass and decorate with a strawberry on the side of the glass. Frost the edge of the glass with fraise and sugar.

Pukka Chukka

1 measure lime juice
Ginger beer

Half fill a highball glass with ice and add the lime juice and then top with ginger beer. Stir well and decorate with a slice of fresh lime or lemon and 2 straws.

Pussyfoot

½ measure lemon juice
½ measure orange juice
½ measure lime juice
1 dash grenadine
1 egg yolk
Soda to top up

Shake ingredients well with ice and strain into a large wine glass. Top with soda. Decorate with a maraschino cherry on a stick and 2 straws.

Rosy Pippin

1 dash grenadine
3 measures apple juice
1 dash lemon juice
Ginger ale

Mix ingredients with ice and pour into a large goblet. Top with ginger ale. Decorate with slices of apple and 2 straws.

St Clements

2 measures orange juice
2 measures bitter lemon

Mix ingredients well with ice and pour into a highball glass. Top up with ice and decorate with slices of orange and lemon with 2 straws.

San Francisco

1 measure orange juice
1 measure lemon juice
1 measure pineapple juice
1 measure grapefruit juice
2 dashes grenadine
1 egg white
Soda to top up

Shake ingredients well with ice and pour into a large goblet. Top with soda and decorate with slices of orange, lemon, lime and pineapple speared with a cherry on a stick and 2 straws.

Shirley Temple

1 measure passion fruit juice
2 measures pineapple juice
Lemonade to top up

Blend the fruit juices with 4–5 cubes of ice until smooth and pour into a highball glass. Top with lemonade. Decorate with a slice of pineapple speared with a cherry on a stick and 2 straws.

Southern Belle

Sprig of mint
1 teaspoon sugar
1 dash lemon juice
Ginger ale

Crush mint and sugar in a mixing glass until the mint is pulverized, then add a dash of lemon juice. Pour into a highball glass full of ice and top up with ginger ale. Decorate with a sprig of mint and 2 straws.

Temperance Mocktail

2 measures lemon juice
2 dashes grenadine
1 egg yolk

Shake ingredients well with ice and strain into a cocktail glass. Decorate with a cherry on a stick.

Ugly

Orange juice
Grapefruit juice

Take a highball glass full of ice and fill half with orange juice and half with grapefruit juice. Pour into a mixing glass and then back into the highball glass. Decorate with a slice of orange and 2 straws.

Virgin Mary

¼ measure lemon juice
Tomato juice
Pinch of salt
Pepper
1 dash Tabasco sauce
1 dash Worcestershire sauce

Fill a large goblet half full of ice and add ingredients. Pour into a mixing glass and back into the goblet; repeat this twice. Decorate with a slice of lemon and a stick of celery.

Waabine Cooler

2 dashes Angostura bitters
1 dash lime juice
Ginger beer

Mix ingredients with ice and pour into a large goblet. Decorate with a wedge of fresh lime and two thin straws.

Zavarone Special

Grenadine
Ginger ale

Fill a champagne glass three-quarters full of ginger ale and then add 5 drops of grenadine. Decorate with a cherry on a stick.

Left to right **Rosy Pippin,
Temperance Mocktail (in front),
San Francisco, Shirley Temple.**

PARTY-TIME

Hints on how to give a cocktail party: what preparations to make beforehand, what drinks to serve and a fund of mouth-watering recipes for canapés and crudités to tempt your guests.

The Cocktail Party

A party specifically for cocktails sounds exciting before it begins; but a tempting spread of appetizers adds that special touch. Here is a choice of recipes from luxurious cones of smoked salmon to simple raw vegetables and dips.

Throwing your first cocktail party can be an unnerving experience, especially when your newly acquired skill at concocting cocktails is put to the test.

Parties need planning. First decide on the number of guests: this should be kept to a minimum of eight people for your first party, to enable you to enjoy their company as well as mix their drinks.

Play safe with a limited number of cocktails. And organize it so that some of the guests help themselves. For instance, a large jug of tomato juice and a few bottles of vodka strategically placed will entice guests into making their own Bloody Marys. A large punch bowl will also do the trick. There are also a number of cocktails which can be prepared beforehand. Martinis, for instance, can be pre-mixed, strained into jugs and kept chilled in the refrigerator until the party starts.

Glasses can be hired, usually from a wine merchant or liquor store. You will need at least two glasses per person as most of the guests will want to try more than one concoction.

A large quantity of ice is required for making cocktails. Either order it from an ice merchant, who will also deliver, or buy it from a local store. Alternatively, make it in the freezer compartment of a refrigerator. Beg, borrow or steal a large insulated container: empty the ice from the ice tray into it and keep it in the refrigerator. Start making the ice at least two days before the party to be sure of having enough.

The cocktail party was originally intended as the overture to a meal, but, nowadays, many people serve a selection of canapés instead. The food and cocktails you choose are determined by the time of day and the occasion. For Sunday brunch parties at midday, why not offer scrambled eggs and bacon with Bloody Marys? Or for more sophisticated fare try champagne cocktails with appetizers of lobster and asparagus.

When serving exotic cocktails which are mainly rum-based and tend to be sweet, do not offer the usual fare of potato chips and olives, since they are too salty. Instead, serve appetizers such as ham rolled round pineapple chunks, grapes stuffed with cream cheese, and canapés of duck pâté and cherries.

Often a host provides too great a range of hors d'oeuvres. For a party of eight to ten, a choice of two cold and one hot canapé is quite sufficient. Allow three or four per person. Alternatively, crudités (raw vegetables) with a selection of dips always proves popular, and is very easy to prepare.

Cocktail parties can be held at any time, sometimes fulfilling their original function as the prelude to a meal, either in the afternoon or evening. The most popular time is the 'happy hour', between six and eight, before the main entertainment of the evening. However, an ideal time for cocktails can be late at night. Here cream cocktails come into their own, especially when accompanied by a late night snack.

Whether your party is held late in the morning, or late at night, remember not to overreach yourself. Keep the number of guests down so that you can be sure of talking easily to all of them and keep the cocktails coming at the same time.

An arrangement of crisp vegetables and a selection of dips provide an enticing accompaniment to a couple of Cool Cucumbers. In front of the vegetables is the Shrimp Dip, while at the back, left to right, are the Tasty Caper Dip, mayonnaise flavoured with tomato purée and, lastly, horseradish.

Crudités and Dips

Crudités

Red Cabbage – Celery – White Cabbage – Carrots – Cucumber – Cauliflower – Radishes – Turnip – Green Beans.

These should be cleaned well and peeled where necessary. Cut into batons of approximately 152 × 19mm (6 × ¾in); this can vary according to whether you wish the crudités to appear as a dainty display or an eye-catching arrangement of raw vegetables.

Guacamole

2 avocados
7cl (2½fl oz or ¼ cup US) sour cream
Black pepper
1 small grated onion
Lemon juice
½ green pepper

Chop and blanch the green pepper. Scoop out flesh from avocados and mix with rest of ingredients to make a coarse purée. Chill and serve with bread sticks, blinis or corn chips.

Madras Dip

2 hardboiled eggs
2 cups sour cream
2 tablespoons mayonnaise
2 teaspoons curry powder
1 teaspoon grated onion
2 tablespoons grated green pepper
2 tablespoons grated celery
Seasoning

Add roughly diced eggs to all other ingredients which have been smoothly blended in a blender. The consistency is thin. Chill, sprinkle with paprika and serve with pappadoms or corn chips.

Russian Dressing

1 can condensed tomato soup
1 cup vinegar
½ cup olive oil
1 clove chopped garlic
1 teaspoon brown sugar
Seasoning
1 small chopped onion

Place all ingredients in a blender and blend until smooth. Serve chilled.

Shrimp Dip

¼ cup milk
1 cup mayonnaise
3 drops Tabasco sauce
1 tablespoon Worcestershire sauce
¼ teaspoon garlic salt
1 small onion, chopped
227g (8oz) cubed cheddar cheese
142g (5oz) can drained shrimps

Place all ingredients in blender and blend until smooth. Serve chilled.

Tasty Caper Dip

¼ cup cream
Seasoning
½ diced onion
227g (8oz) cream cheese
1 tablespoon anchovy paste
1 teaspoon capers
1 teaspoon caraway seeds

Blend cream, cheese, anchovy paste and seasoning together until smooth. Add the other ingredients and stir until thoroughly mixed.

For other dips use plain mayonnaise, horseradish sauce or tartare sauce. A tablespoon of tomato sauce can be mixed in with the mayonnaise to give it a different flavour.

Canapés

The bases for the following canapé recipes may be made from either pastry, toast, savoury biscuits or crackers. They become soggy if left too long so prepare them as close to the time of serving as possible.

Californian Canapés

8–10 bases
77g (2¾oz) demi-sel or cream cheese
28g (1oz) butter
1 tablespoon hot milk
Redcurrant jelly

Mix cheese and butter together and add enough hot milk to make a piping consistency. Pipe in a circle around the edge of the base. Fill the centre with redcurrant jelly.

Gruyère Canapés

4 slices white bread
Butter
113g (4oz) grated Gruyère
8 anchovy fillets, finely chopped
3 tablespoons mayonnaise
4 tablespoons (⅓ cup US) grated Parmesan
Paprika

Toast bread on one side only. Spread untoasted side with butter. Mix remaining ingredients, except paprika, together. Spread on buttered side. Place on baking sheet in very hot oven (475°F, 245°C, Gas 9) for 5 mins. Remove, cut each slice into 6 and sprinkle with paprika. Serve immediately.

Plantain Chips

Not quite a canapé, but an unusual appetizer.

1 plantain
West Indian hot pepper sauce

The plantain should not be too black. Cut both ends off and peel. Cut the plantain in half and then slice lengthways. The slices should be 12mm (½in) thick. Deep fry in hot oil until golden brown, about 5 minutes. The edges should be crispy. Serve with a little hot pepper sauce and salt.

Roquefort and Brandy Canapés

16 small bases
113g (4oz) Roquefort cheese
2 tablespoons dry white wine
1 tablespoon brandy
Butter
Cayenne
Chopped olives or parsley to garnish

Break cheese into small pieces and process in a blender with wine and brandy. Chill. Spread bases with a little butter and then spread on cheese mixture. Sprinkle with chives.

Dreamy dips and mouth-watering canapés to go with the cocktails – minty green Jade and the whisky-based Trinity. Top to bottom The Mexican avocado dip: Guacamole, redcurrant-centred Californian Canapés, Gruyère Canapés, the curry-flavoured Madras Dip and Stuffed Olive Canapés.

As an accompaniment to an Adonis, garnished with an orange twist, serve, top to bottom, Fanchouettes in their oval cases, delicious pâté Bouchées à la Strasbourg, Savoury Puffs and Tartlets Niçoise with a choice of three fillings.

Salmon spread de luxe

½kg (1lb) fresh poached salmon
1 cup mayonnaise
2 tablespoons diced green pepper
2 tablespoons diced red pimento
2 teaspoons lemon juice
1 teaspoon tarragon vinegar
1 teaspoon horseradish cream
1 teaspoon chopped dried dill
Seasoning

Remove skin and bones from salmon and chop very finely. Put mayonnaise and pepper and pimento into a blender on low until smooth. Turn into bowl with the rest of the ingredients and mix well. Chill. Serve with brown bread, blinis or use as a filling for bouchées.

Smoked Cod's Roe and Salted Almonds

8–10 bases
106g (3¾oz) jar smoked cod's roe
14g (½oz) butter
2 tablespoons thick cream
Salted almonds to garnish

Blend cod's roe, butter and cream until smooth and then pipe on to the base. Decorate with a salted almond.

Smoked Salmon and Cream Cheese Canapés

85g (3oz) cream cheese
Seasoning
1 tablespoon hot milk
56g (2oz) smoked salmon
Lemon juice
Black pepper
Parsley to garnish

Work cheese, seasoning and milk to a piping consistency. Season the smoked salmon with lemon juice and black pepper and chop into fine dice. Pipe cheese onto bases. Sprinkle the chopped salmon on top. Garnish with a sprig of parsley.

Stuffed Olive Canapés

8 bases
8 large pitted olives
8 anchovy fillets

Filling
28g (1oz) butter
1 teaspoon chutney
1 hardboiled egg, sieved
Seasoning

Mix all filling ingredients to a smooth paste and spread a little on each base. Curl an anchovy fillet around each base. Fill olives with filling by pressing it in with a knife and place the olive in the centre of the base. Garnish with a sprig of parsley.

Savoury Pastries

Anchovy Pirouski

113g (4oz) pastry as used in Tartlets Niçoise below
1 small onion, finely chopped
2 tablespoons butter
2–3 cups cooked diced potatoes
10 anchovy fillets, finely chopped
Seasoning
1 beaten egg to glaze

Sauté onion in the butter until lightly coloured, then combine with the rest of the ingredients. Roll out pastry and cut into 76mm (3in) rounds. Place a drop of mixture on one side of each round and fold and seal. Brush with beaten egg and bake in a very hot oven (475°F, 245°C, Gas 9) until brown. Serve hot.

As a variation, cooked rice can be substituted for potatoes and ground beef for anchovies.

Blinis

3 tablespoons (¼ cup US) oil
3 large eggs
20cl (7fl oz) water
1 heaped cup wholewheat flour
¾ cup white (all-purpose) flour
2 teaspoons baking powder
1 teaspoon salt

Place all the ingredients in blender and mix to a smooth batter. Heat a frying pan with a little oil until a haze appears. Drop a few tablespoons of batter into the pan and cook until brown on both sides. Keep warm for serving with one of the following dips.

★A spoonful of sour cream mixed with chopped chives.

★Make bacon rolls, cut blini around the bacon roll and spear with a cocktail stick.

★A spoonful of pâté on each blini and fold over.

Bouchées à la Strasbourg

10 cocktail vol-au-vent cases
Pâté de foie gras in a tube
Slices of stuffed olive

Discard tops of pastry cases and fill cases with pâté. Garnish with a slice of olive.

Bouchées Ecossaises

10 cocktail vol-au-vent cases
70g (2½oz) demi-sel or cream cheese
1 tablespoon thick cream
85g (3oz) smoked salmon, shredded
Black pepper
Lemon juice

Mix cheese, cream, salmon, lemon juice and seasoning together and fill the vol-au-vent cases.

Bouchées Russes

10 cocktail vol-au-vent cases
56g (2oz) cream cheese
50g (1¾oz) Danish caviar

Discard tops from pastry cases. Fill with cheese and garnish with a little caviar.

Creamed Salmon and Shrimp Vol-au-vent

42g (1½oz) butter
28g (1oz or ¼ cup US) flour
4 tablespoons dry vermouth
Salt and pepper
28cl (½ pint or 1¼ cups US) milk
3–4 tablespoons (¼–⅓ cup US) thick cream
170g (6oz) cooked or canned salmon
56g (2oz) peeled shrimps
2 hardboiled eggs, diced
20 cocktail vol-au-vent cases

Cook onions gently in butter until soft but uncoloured (about 5 minutes). Add flour and cook for 2 minutes, stirring. Remove from heat, add milk, vermouth and seasoning and bring to the boil, stirring until the sauce thickens. Fold in cream, salmon, shrimps and egg. Fill vol-au-vent cases (already cooked) with this mixture. Put into a moderate oven (350°F, 175°C, Gas 4) and heat for a few minutes.

Fanchouettes

10 oval pastry cases
1 breast of chicken, cooked
½ red pepper
½ green pepper
4 tablespoons mayonnaise
1 hardboiled egg and parsley to garnish

Dice chicken finely and add peppers, which should have been chopped and blanched beforehand. Add enough mayonnaise to blend. Fill pastry cases and garnish each with a slice of hardboiled egg and a sprig of parsley.

91

A simpler assortment of
appetizers go well with the
refreshing Harvey Wallbanger (in
the tall tumbler) and the
enchanting Tequila Sunrises. Top
to bottom **Stuffed Tomatoes** with
their hats on, **Stuffed Eggs**,
Cucumber Appetizers sprinkled
with caviar, and **Ham and Cream
Cheese Rolls**.

Savoury Puffs
14cl (¼ pint or ⅔ cup US) water
56g (2oz) butter
70g (2½oz or large ½ cup US) flour
Seasoning
Pinch of cayenne
2 eggs
Parmesan, grated
Beaten egg

Put water and butter in a pan. Sift flour and seasoning onto a piece of paper. Bring contents of pan to boil. When boiling, remove the pan and quickly add the flour and seasoning. Beat well until smooth, then beat in 2 eggs and continue beating until smooth. Place mixture in piping bag and pipe small balls on to a damp baking sheet. Brush with beaten egg and sprinkle with Parmesan cheese. Bake for 12 minutes in a very hot oven (475°F, 245°C, Gas 9), or until crisp. Remove and allow to cool.

Fillings
Use one of the following, and fill at the last possible moment.

★28g (1oz) cream cheese
   1 tablespoon chopped celery
   1 tablespoon chopped green pepper
   1 tablespoon chopped chives
   1 teaspoon tomato ketchup
   Seasoning

Mix together and season well, adding a little cream if desired.

★28g (1oz) cream cheese
   Seasoning
   Lemon juice
   1 tablespoon cream
   56g (2oz) potted shrimps

Mix the first 4 ingredients together and garnish with shrimps.

★85g (3oz) chicken, finely diced
   1 tablespoon mayonnaise
   28g (1oz) cooked tongue, finely chopped
   Parsley

Blend well together and garnish with chopped parsley

Tartlets Niçoise
113g (4oz or 1 cup US) flour
Seasoning
Cayenne
56g (2oz) shortening
14g (½oz) grated Parmesan
½ egg yolk mixed with 1 tablespoon water

Sift flour with seasoning, rub or cut in shortening, add cheese, and mix to a dough with egg yolk and water. Chill for 30 minutes, roll out thinly and line 16 tart moulds. Bake blind for 8 minutes in a moderate oven (350°F, 175°C, Gas 4).

Fillings
★1 clove garlic
   56g (2oz) unsalted butter
   Seasoning
   Sugar
   Lemon juice
   1 teaspoon tomato purée
   2 tablespoons chopped parsley
   and chopped almonds to garnish

Cream butter and garlic together and add rest of ingredients. Mix well. Fill pastry cases with mixtures and garnish with chopped parsley and almonds.

★56g (2oz) curd or cream cheese
   14g (½oz) butter
   Seasoning
   4 black olives, finely chopped
   1 hardboiled egg to garnish

Mix cheese, butter and seasoning well together; add the chopped olives and fill pastry cases. Garnish with chopped egg yolk on one side and chopped egg white on the other.

★56g (2oz) can sardines
   1 teaspoon chopped capers
   Vinaigrette
   Tomato to garnish

Drain sardines and scrape off skin, remove tail and mash with the capers and a little vinaigrette. Fill the pastry cases and garnish with tomato slices.

Cones, Rolls and Stuffings

Cucumber Appetizers
Danish red lumpfish roe
1 cucumber
170g (6oz) cream cheese
1 small carton (⅔ cup US) sour cream
Seasoning
Vinegar

Peel cucumber and cut into 38mm (1½in) slices. Scoop out seeds with teaspoon leaving a layer at the bottom to make a pot. Soak in vinegar for 2–3 hours, then drain and dry. Mix cheese and cream together and fill pots. Top with lumpfish roe.

Ham and Cream Cheese Rolls
227g (½lb) sliced ham
142g (5oz) demi-sel or cream cheese
1 tablespoon hot milk
Seasoning
½ dill cucumber, chopped
Dash of paprika
Celery to garnish

Cut slices of ham in half diagonally. Work rest of ingredients together. Place a teaspoon of the mixture on each piece of ham and roll into a cone. Fasten with a cocktail stick and serve garnished with fresh celery.

Salt Beef Rolls
113g (¼lb) cooked salt beef, sliced very thin
56g (2oz) curd or cream cheese
Horseradish sauce
Cocktail onions to garnish

Spread slices of beef with cheese and horseradish. Roll up and fasten with a cocktail stick.

Saumon Fumée à la Moscovite
Smoked salmon
Caviar

Roll slices of salmon into cones and fill with caviar.

Stuffed Eggs
12 hardboiled eggs
1 tablespoon mayonnaise
1 tablespoon cream
Seasoning
½ teaspoon anchovy flavouring
Parsley to garnish

Cut eggs in half lengthwise and remove yolks. Press through sieve and combine with other ingredients. Refill eggs and garnish with a sprig of parsley.

Stuffed Tomatoes
8 medium tomatoes
Seasoning
227g (8oz) frozen shrimps, chopped
28cl (½ pint or 1¼ cups US) mayonnaise

Cut off the tops of the tomatoes and scoop out the insides which can be discarded. Mix shrimps with mayonnaise and seasoning. Fill the tomatoes and replace their tops.

Index

Terms in constant use in the recipes are not entered each time in the index. The reader is referred to where they appear in 'Basics' and the introduction to each group of cocktail recipes. Entries in italic refer to illustrations and in bold indicate the recipes.

Acknowledgements
The publishers would like to
thank the following people
and organizations for their
contributions to the book:

Kenneth Abbott Ltd, Rum
Distributors, 7 Cork Street,
London W1.
John E. Fells & Sons Ltd,
Wine Merchants, 56 Tooley
Street, London SE1.
J. B. Reynier Ltd, Wine
Merchants, 16 Tachbrook
Street, London SW1.
Chinacraft at Page's, 87–91
Shaftesbury Avenue,
London W1.
Rumours, 33 Wellington
Street, London WC2.
Zanzibar, 30 Great Queen
Street, London WC2.
Brian Jones, for his cocktail
food recipes.